Willa Cather's
Transforming Vision

Willa Cather's Transforming Vision

New France and the American Northeast

Gary Brienzo

Selinsgrove: Susquehanna University Press
London and Toronto: Associated University Presses

Associated University Presses
440 Forsgate Drive
Cranbury, NJ 08512

Associated University Presses
25 Sicilian Avenue
London WC1A 2QH, England

Associated University Presses
P.O. Box 338, Port Credit
Mississauga, Ontario
Canada L5G 4L8

The paper used in this publication meets the requirements
of the American National Standard for Permanence of Paper
for Printed Library Materials Z39.48-1984.

Excerpts from *Shadows on a Rock* by Willa Cather copyright 1931 by Willa Cather and renewed 1959 by the Executors of the Estate of Willa Cather, Reprinted by permission of Alfred A. Knopf, Inc.

Excerpts from *Death Comes for the Archbishop* by Willa Cather copyright 1929 by Willa Cather and renewed 1957 by Edith Lewis and the City Bank Farmers Trust Co. Reprinted by permission of Alfred A. Knopf, Inc.

Excerpts from *Willa Cather: A Literary Life* by James Woodress and *The Voyage Perilous: Willa Cather's Romanticism* are reprinted with permission of the University of Nebraska Press.

Library of Congress Cataloging-in-Publication Data

Brienzo, Gary, 1954–
    Willa Cather's transforming vision : New France and the American
Northeast / Gary Brienzo.
        p.   cm.
    Includes bibliographical references (p.   ) and index.
    ISBN 0-945636-66-0 (alk. paper)
    1. Cather, Willa, 1873–1947—Criticism and interpretation.
    2. Historical fiction, American—History and criticism.   3. New
France—In literature.   4. Northeastern States—In literature.
    I. Title.
PS3505.A87Z5836   1995
813'.52—dc20   94-17434
                                                                          CIP

Contents

Willa Cather's
Transforming Vision

1

Cather's Literary and Personal Search

Biographers of Willa Cather have long recognized the importance of the American Northeast and adjacent New France to this writer, although literary critics haven't paid the region much attention, focusing instead upon Nebraska and, secondarily, the Southwest. Despite such oversights, the literary influence of the region is obvious in Cather's story of seventeenth-century Quebec, *Shadows on the Rock*, (1931) and in one of her final works, "Before Breakfast," a story published posthumously in *The Old Beauty and Others* (1948). As well as these stories set completely in the region, Cather peopled many of her other works with characters, originating from New England—from Jim Burden's inspirational teacher, Gaston Cleric, in *My Ántonia* (1918), to the Maine native Nat Wheeler in *One of Ours* (1922), to Evangeline Knightly in Cather's last completed story, "The Best Years." Losing more and more of her filial ties to the Red Cloud, Nebraska, home that inspired so many of her greatest works of fiction, Cather turned increasingly to other regions for the "quiet centre of life" that Sarah Orne Jewett advised her to find in order to complete herself as an artist.[1] As a number of her letters and works attest, the American Southwest was an important, almost mythically regenerative place for Cather; so was the France she often praised above all other countries. Only to the Northeast of this country, however, rich with French and American pioneering influences, did she return consistently for most of her adult life.

Many explanations have been offered for the powerful affinity Cather felt for the region, from her longing to escape the Nebraska Plains she once described as "a country as bare as a piece of sheet iron,"[2] to her desire to become part of the established literary and cultural traditions she associated with the Northeast. James Woodress, in his biography, *Willa Cather, A Literary Life*, explains Cather's connection to the area as one of the "several dichotomies in her life," a strong pulling "back to the [northeastern] hills and mountains" that recalled for Cather her earliest Virginia home, "despite her acquired affection for the prairie."[3] Woodress underscores Cather's nostalgia for the mountains of the East in describing her eagerness to move to Pittsburgh. "Among the several polarities that pulled at Cather all her life," he writes, "was the attraction of the eastern mountains against the tug of the prairie of her adopted state."[4]

An explanation of Cather's sense of belonging in the Northeast, offered by the woman with whom she shared most of her adult life, makes Cather's regional affinity even more obvious. In *Willa Cather Living: A Personal Record*, Edith Lewis writes that

> of all the places Willa Cather knew and enjoyed during her life . . . Jaffrey [New Hampshire] became the one she found best to work in. The fresh, pine-scented woods and pastures, with their multitudinous wild flowers, the gentle skies, the little enclosed fields, had in them nothing of the disturbing, exalting, impelling memories and associations of the past—her own past. Each day there was like an empty canvas, a clean sheet of paper to be filled. She lived with a simple sense of physical well-being, of weather, and of country solitude.[5]

Lewis expands on the attraction of solitude to Cather when she describes the even stronger ties Cather developed for the island off the coast of New Brunswick, Grand Manan. "Here was solitude without loneliness," she writes, and "although there were a good many physical discomforts to put up with, the quiet, the great remove from all mundane things, and the natural loveliness of the place made Grand Manan, in the summer, a better place to work than any other Willa Cather had found."[6] Lewis makes the Northeast's hold on Cather even stronger, saying that, in the summer of 1928, after her father's death, "I remember how, that summer, Grand Manan seemed the only foothold left on earth."[7] Two other biographers, E. K. Brown and Leon Edel, add that Cather's "stays on the island were intended to be a rest from the traffic and telephones of Manhattan, and its heat and harassments. . . . It was at Grand Manan . . . that Willa Cather found the nearest equivalent to her stays in Red Cloud."[8]

Considering this extensive biographical treatment, the lack of an overall critical interpretation of the northern region's symbolic significance in Cather's fiction is indeed surprising. Among some interpretive theories already propounded, critics posit two additional attractions of New France and the Northeast besides pristine scenery and solitude for an author from the newly settled West. First, as well as the personal homesickness for the East described, the general nostalgia in an aspiring writer and early devotee of Henry James for a national culture or civilization also seems natural. For Cather, this longing was fulfilled during her voyages to New England while working on assignment for S. S. McClure, during which time Cather met Mrs. Annie Fields, and through her, as Cather herself wrote later, "'the great shades'" of the literary past. Throughout her distinguished career, Fields had known Dickens, Thackeray, and Arnold, as well as American literary giants like Hawthorne, Emerson, Lowell, Holmes, and Longfellow. Becoming acquainted with Fields herself was significant for Cather, who wrote of the meeting that at last "an American of the Apache period and territory could come to inherit a Colonial past."[9] The encounter has assumed heightened importance in recent years, with scholars like Sharon O'Brien attributing nothing less to the relationship than "Cather's cultural acquisition" made possible by "Mrs. Fields' ability to connect past and present, European and American culture."[10]

Even more importantly, it was while visiting Mrs. Fields at 148 Charles Street that Cather met the woman who many maintain was to have the greatest effect on her early career, Sarah Orne Jewett. In such company, and appreciating America's literary heritage as never before, Cather told Jewett that for the first time she felt Americans indeed had a past and culture of their own, and that she had gone away feeling exultant.[11] Cather's second revelation about the region, according to Edith Lewis, was a similar shock of cultural recognition which came with Cather's "discovery" of Quebec City's religious and historical legacy in North America. Lewis described Cather's first impression on seeing Quebec in the most superlative terms she knew, calling it no less than "her discovery of France on this continent," with "its extraordinarily French character, isolated and kept intact through hundreds of years, as if by a miracle, on this great un-French continent."[12]

Later scholars and biographers were to make much of Cather's two discoveries in the region, from Josphine Donovan and Sharon O'Brien tracing Cather's emerging matriarchal literary voices to the friends at 148 Charles Street, to John J. Murphy's naming Quebec City "'mon centre . . . mon paradis terrestre'" for Cather.[13] Her love of the literary and domestic artistries that she was to see exemplified in the cradles of American and Canadian civilization was to remain with Cather throughout her entire life, finding ultimate expression in her only long work set completely in the region, *Shadows*. Cather herself could not praise domestic art, particularly as practiced by the French and French Canadians, too highly. The Frenchman, she once told an interviewer,

> doesn't talk nonsense about art, about self-expression; he is too greatly occupied with building the things that make his home. His house, his garden, his vineyards, these are the things that fill his mind. He creates something beautiful, something lasting. And what happens? When a French painter wants to paint a picture he makes a copy of a garden, a home, a village. The art in them inspires his brush. And twenty, thirty, forty years later you'll come to see the original of that picture, and you'll find it, changed only by the mellowness of time. Restlessness such as ours, success such as ours, striving such as ours, do not make for beauty. Other things must come first; good cookery; cottages that are homes, not playthings; gardens; repose. These are first-rate things, and out of first-rate stuff is art made.[14]

Years later, after Cather had discovered Quebec, she praised the French Canadians for exactly these same traits, and for their adherence to their cultural heritage. "She likes the French Canadians because they have remained practically unchanged for over two hundred years," Louise Bogan of *The New Yorker* wrote in an interview of Cather, "Quebec because it is built to last, and because its buildings show the influence of French architects of France's best period. Its inhabitants like good food and simple pleasures."[15] Shortly after the publication of *Shadows*, and in response to Connecticut governor Wilbur Cross's sympathetic review of the novel in *The Saturday Review of Literature*, Cather even more strongly expressed her view of the seriousness of domestic art as exemplified in her story of New France, and of its close ties to all other artistic achievements. She wrote to the governor:

> An orderly little French household that went on trying to live decently ... interests me more than Indian raids or the wild life in the forests ... once having adopted a tone so definite, once having taken your seat in the close air by the apothecary's fire, you can't explode into military glory, any more than you can pour champagne into a salad dressing. ... And really, a new society begins with the salad dressing more than with the destruction of Indian villages.[16]

In addition to Cather's own statements, her friends and critics also point to the growing importance of domesticity in Cather's art, and to the special significance of French and French Canadian culture in the development of this artistry. Lewis stresses the contribution of Cather's French cook, Josephine Bourda, to Cather's life and craft, writing:

> Josephine's father had kept a well-known restaurant near Pau, and she herself was a splendid cook, so that at 5 Bank Street we were able to give a great many dinner-parties. She was an important figure in our lives at that time—high-spirited, warm-hearted, impulsive, brimming over with vitality, and intelligent, as the French are; with great humour, very quick perceptions about people, a rather merciless philosophy of life. She would never speak English, and we were forced to speak our very lame French with her. Her personality was so pervasive and uncompromising that she created a sort of French household atmosphere around us; and I think there is no question that this contributed, to a certain extent, to such novels as *Death Comes for the Archbishop* and *Shadows on the Rock*.[17]

Cather's own accounts of writing *Shadows* also acknowledge Josephine's impact on the novel, a traditional knowledge of French domestic arts that combined with Cather's familiarity with the Northeast to create her stylistically colored yet humanly believable New France. In her personal correspondence at the time, Cather described how she had unconsciously learned the traditional French housekeeping depicted in the novel from Josephine. Her letter to Zoe Akins, written shortly after the book's publication, credited her cook for Cather's own knowledge of French pots, pans, and general household economics.[18] Yet as important as the firsthand knowledge of traditional French domesticity in this northern settlement is, the novel's beautifully stark setting, as unique to the region as the culture of the characters Cather envisions, is equally central to *Shadows*.

Sensing this, critics point out the growing link between the area and Cather's artistic vision, with Hermione Lee celebrating Cather's "recent pleasure in the Grand Manan, Bay of Fundy seascape . . . and the dramatic setting of Quebec itself" as an "intensely beautiful . . . feeling [that] fills the book,"[19] and Woodress finding her descriptions of forests and seascapes as owing "a lot to the five summers she spent on Grand Manan."[20] Two other authors, Marian Marsh Brown and Ruth Crone, devoted an entire volume, *Only One Point of the Compass: Willa Cather in the Northeast*, to Cather's time spent in the region and its impact on her fiction. And Robert J. Nelson's *Willa Cather and France: In Search of the Lost Language*, though not dealing specifically with the cultural or physical details of the Northeast, indirectly touches on both in his discussion of *Shadows*. In New France, Nelson sees Cécile and, through his union with her, Pierre Charron as becoming part of a unified, comforting order to Cather, by dint of their producing four sons who will share their parents' proper blend of Old and New World traits.[21]

In such a reconciliation of connecting influences on Cather's life and fiction, the wisdom of Sarah Orne Jewett increasingly becomes the point of convergence for the younger writer. As well as contributing to Cather's best fiction, that which bears her own artistic voice, Jewett's affectionate admonitions helped form Cather's beliefs about what made life worth living, including her ideas of how and where to live. Jewett's advice was so important because it complemented ideas Cather herself was forming about the domestic qualities that enhanced life. Jewett wrote Cather:

I cannot help saying what I think about your writing and its being hindered by such incessant, important, responsible work as you have in your hands now [as a magazine editor] . . . if you don't keep and guard and mature your force, and above all, have time and quiet to perfect your work, you will be writing things not much better than you did five years ago. . . . Your vivid, exciting companionship in the office must not be your audience, you must find your own quiet centre of life, and write from that to the world.[22]

The fiction Cather wrote after reading these words suggests how thoroughly Jewett's words and example helped her to seek her own balance and to reconcile disparate forces in her life, so that this self-described "American of the Apache period" could truly feel part of a larger literary tradition. Jewett's guidance was great enough, to critical biographers like Sharon O'Brien, to make the impetuous younger writer, "imbued with Romantic ideology, convinced that the artist must be male," and who previously "perceived no artistry in woman's domestic work, no links between herself and a female culture," come to recognize, "after meeting Sarah Orne Jewett in 1908 . . . that even a literary art could be communal and selfless."[23] O'Brien characterizes Jewett's artistry as "inspired by love for her Maine homeland and its residents" and marked by a "creativity as preservation as well as self-expression, similar to the farm wife's work or the storyteller's art, more closely related to folk culture than was the fiction of Cather's first mentor, Henry James."[24]

Jewett offered Cather an alternative literary tradition to James's legacy, a vision that encompassed previously overlooked settings and subjects. O'Brien describes this vision as "an American and a female literary tradition,"[25] one which does not view artistry as "inconsistent with qualities and tasks conventionally considered feminine," and which embraces Mrs. Todd's creativity as one "expressed in her knowledge of herbs, spices, and the ancient female art of healing."[26] Parallels between Cather and Jewett are many, and they have been described in anti-industrial, feminist, and even religious terms— for example, as a matriarchal Christianity shared by the two authors.[27] Even stronger connections between Cather and Jewett are possible, particularly in the force of their most memorable female heroes. As Helen Fiddyment Levy has pointed out, the domestic home place created by Cather, Jewett, and others, often bears the imprint of semidivine wise women, women like Jewett's Mrs. Todd and Mrs. Blackett and Cather's Ántonia Shimerda and, in her way, Cécile Auclair.[28] More than merely informing individual works of fiction, such characters help define a nation's literature. "Through the creation of the home place and the evocation of a semi-divine wise woman," Fiddyment Levy writes, "[women writers] hope to offer an alternate imaginative narrative of American beginnings, one which challenges the legends of the womanless woodsman moving ever farther away from woman and home."[29]

As well as strong thematic ties, equally potent stylistic bonds also unite Cather and Jewett. In *New England Local Color Literature: A Women's Tradition*, Josephine Donovan, in addition to describing the artists' spiritual kinship, considers a shared "imaginative realism" in which

> the writer deals not just with the facts of the story but rather uses those facts to point out a dimension beyond the real ... it is writing that stirs one's imagination, that makes one dream. And it is the kind of writing that Jewett bequeathed to her protegée, Willa Cather.[30]

This passage echoes other comparisons between Cather and Jewett, including their emulation of Flaubert. Jewett is known to have pinned an epigraph over her desk which to some is as apt a description of Cather's aims as of Jewett's. In any case, few words would seem more illuminating for *Death Comes for the Archbishop* or for *Shadows*. The quote borrowed from Flaubert reads: "'Ce n'est pas de faire rire ni de faire pleurer, ni de vous mettre à fureur, mais d'agir à la façon de la nature, c'est à dire de faire rêver.'"[31] The words evoke what might in Jewett's case be called an "imaginative realism," as they describe the color-laden, detailed description of the Quebec of Cather's *Shadows*. They also go beyond realism to an American Romanticism that Josephine Donovan describes as the transformation of "a spiritual landscape, a metaphorical realm," into the artist's written expression of "her vision of the human condition."[32]

In this definition as well as in her extending of conclusions about a communal world of strong women to the realm of matriarchal Christianity, Donovan moves to an analysis similar to Susan J. Rosowski's interpretations of *Shadows*. Both critics' approaches seem particularly convincing in considering the role of Cécile Auclair in the novel and in the healthiness of women characters living in Christian communion as opposed to the destruction of recluses like Cather's Jeanne Le Ber or Jewett's Joanna. "The local colorists' great accomplishment, indeed, was that they did not remain negatively fixed upon the destructive practices of patriarchal society," Donovan writes; "rather they created a positive, other world of their own that promoted powerful and independent women."³³ Donovan says that Jewett went further, to the creation of "an authentically female-identified vision of her own" and "a woman's vision of transcendence" that could overcome patriarchal domination and create a "supportive community of women, sustained by a kind of matriarchal Christianity, and by traditions of women's lore and culture."³⁴

The importance of a woman-centered Christian community in Jewett's fiction is clear, especially when the beneficence of characters like Mrs. Blackett or Mrs. Todd is considered. Nowhere is the strength of this community more plainly seen in Jewett's fiction than in the contrast between these successful domestic artists and the ruined "Poor Joanna" Todd. It is this contrast that Donovan says creates

> the tension between individualism and the participation of the self in a community identity. The former is seen positively in a series of spinsters who prefer to live alone, but is regarded as destructive by Jewett when it is carried to an extreme. The importance of a transcending community is stressed in the late works. It is a community primarily of women and sustained by a kind of matriarchal Christianity and by other traditions of women's lore.³⁵

Joanna, part of no such community, is a recluse from both human and divine company. She remains, in Donovan's words, "one of Jewett's extreme isolates, who seems to culminate the local color tradition of Calvinist [patriarchal] oppression," hiding herself on her island home "out of a sense of Calvinistic self-flagellation for having committed the 'unpardonable sin' of blaspheming God in the wake of her disappointment" at an unrequited love.[36] To another critic, Margaret Roman, Joanna goes so far as to deny her female inheritance and to adopt "a narrow, rigid male vision" of an unforgiving God who dooms her to solitude.[37] Seen in these ways, Joanna is the saddest of characters, neither part of a secular matriarchal community nor a religious one.

In *Shadows*, Cather similarly creates foils to the domestic integration that forms the heart of her work. Quebec comes to stand for a society grounded in domestic traditions passed through the generations in a matriarchal line of descent. The matriarchal, even Marian structure of the community of Quebec, especially as it contrasts to the patriarchal Calvinism that menaced Jewett and the local colorists, has not been missed by scholars.[38] Such views gain credibility in light of Cather when she mutes one of the most important aspects of seventeenth-century Quebec's history, the military campaigns of the governor general, Count Frontenac. Cather made plain how little she cared for the "military glory" and "Indian raids" and how she preferred the "salad dressing" of a developing civilization, as has been noted in her letter to Governor Cross.[39] To Susan Rosowski in *The Voyage Perilous: Willa Cather's Romanticism*, as much as to Donovan in her interpretation of Jewett, the creation of order and a sense of community is possible because of "the power of domestic ritual." Such power not only enhances the Auclairs' personal life but also forms the "domestic actions that knit together the colonists and enable them to survive."[40]

Other critics view women's domestic contributions as playing an equally powerful role in the unification and prosperity of their communities. The civic structures of New World settlements are shaped by domestic influences to Fiddyment Levy, who sees Cather and other women writers as making of the home place "a metaphoric representative of democratic egalitarianism and community action" and "a purer vision of American democracy" that rejects "the repressive hierarchy of the earlier paternalistic family."[41] Similarly, Merrill M. Skaggs sees in the rituals, both domestic and sacred, of the Quebec of *Shadows* a "stability and undisrupted cultural continuity"[42] essential to life, and Margaret Roman, in describing Jewett's domestic fiction and its influences on other writers, sees non-gender bound, equal communities as marked by "a healthy progress in which human beings move forward by living the life of their choice commingled with a compassionate connection to others."[43]

Other, still more specific, domestic arts, including the power of healing for which Jewett's Mrs. Todd is best known, also form the core of Cather's most fully expressed domestic work, *Shadows*. Among those who are healed in the book are the abandoned child Jacques, the injured woodsman Frichette, and the maimed torturer Blinker. To Rosowski, all are drawn to Cécile's kitchen, representing "our most basic human fears of being lost, abandoned, tormented," before each is healed. "Jacques is washed, clothed, and instructed," Rosowski writes; "Frichette is fed; and Blinker is solaced."[44] Even more importantly, these examples illustrate how much of the domestic ritual that heals individuals and binds communities in both Cather's and Jewett's fiction is bound up in storytelling, from Mrs. Todd and Mrs. Fosdick telling the narrator about "poor Joanna" in *The Country of the Pointed Firs*, to the healing and soothing tales that are shared around the Auclair hearth and which enrich *Shadows*.

Not surprisingly, fire, often as a necessary ingredient in the successful telling of stories, also becomes a domestic symbol that joins individuals and communities in the fiction of both Cather and Jewett. The story of Jewett's recluse Joanna is told by the lifelong friends Mrs. Todd and Mrs. Fosdick to their new friend, the narrator of the *Country of the Pointed Firs*, around the narrator's Franklin stove, as "a chilly night of cold northeasterly rain" storms around them. As if completing the new circle of domesticity and friendship, the narrator says that this night marks the first time she has lighted the fire in her room, and so, almost as if in celebration, she has "begged [her] two housemates to come in and keep [her] company."[45] Similarly, many shared stories in *Shadows* are told around the Auclairs' fire, and in the face of a hostile Quebec winter. These tales range from the accounts of Le Ber's angelic visitations, to Euclide Auclair's comforting first of the tormented Blinker and then of the injured Frichette, each of whom tells his story of personal loss and then finds a kind of absolution.[46]

As such illustrations make clear, religious undertones are an important part of the internal story structure of *Shadows*. Cécile playfully demands a story about Mother Catherine from the woman who knew her best, Mother Juschereau, in one of the best examples of the domestic ritual of storytelling in the novel. As the nun is seated with her sprained foot on a stool, surrounded by "scraps of bright silk and velvet sheets of coloured paper" with which she makes artificial flowers for rural parishes, Cécile pleads, "'It has been a long while since you told me a story, Reverend Mother,'" to which the nun laughingly replies, "'Perhaps I have no more to tell you. You must know them all by this time.'" Cécile persists, underscoring the importance of storytelling in her relationship with the religious she knows so well. "'But there is no end to the stories about Mother Catherine de Saint-Augustin,'" she demands. "'I can never hear them all.'" Admitting that her own love of these stories is as strong as the child's, the usually briskly efficient mother superior relents, saying, "'True enough, when you speak her name, the stories come. Since I have had to sit here with my sprain, I have been recalling some of the things she used to tell me herself, when I was not much older than you.'"[47]

The pattern of storytelling Cather employs in *Shadows* seems strikingly like the method Jewett used to great advantage and shows her further indebtedness to her mentor for her choice of subject as well as for her treatment of characters within her narratives. In praising the way Jewett develops characters through her narrative structures, Sharon O'Brien writes that

> Jewett's women rise most fully to artistry . . . in the stories they tell, either about themselves or, more frequently, about other women whose stories they want to pass on. . . . Jewett dramatizes not only the connections between story tellers and listeners but also those between unconscious women artists and conscious ones.[48]

Considered in this way, one of Cather's least recognized female heroes, Cécile Auclair, can be viewed more favorably. By her own frequent telling of stories, not about herself but about other, often legendary women of New France like Mother Catherine or Jeanne Le Ber or even, to the young Cécile, her own mother, Cécile quickly becomes one of Cather's exemplary domestic artists, despite her youth.

She is so marvelously precocious a keeper of domestic order in the new colony that Rosowski, in writing of her accomplishments, acclaims her not simply "a young version of those widely diverse women in Cather's writing who create art from life: Ántonia Cuzak, Marian Forrester, Myra Henshawe, Mrs. James T. Fields," but the most highly developed domestic artist among them. "None compares to Cécile," Rosowski writes. "Cécile is younger, yet more competent and committed than her predecessors: she has the selflessness of her mother . . . which she charges with a passionate dedication to domestic details." Rosowski goes further in her assessment of Cécile as Cather's consummate, if not most realistically developed, domestic artist, concluding that "Cather makes no pretense at presenting childhood as it is lived in the real world; instead, in *Shadows on the Rock* she wrote a saint's life to tell of the apotheosis of a French girl into a Canadian Holy Mother."[49] Rosowski points to Cécile's youth, like Mary's, as "a time of purification," composed of "spiritually cleansing disciplines [which are] repeated until they have become rituals which prepare Cécile for assuming Motherhood." To conclude this metaphor, Rosowski traces Cécile's development in relation to the nurturing she gives the fatherless Jacques, defining her role as a mediator for the child, as Mary is considered the mediator between God and Humanity. She culminates her discussion of Cécile as a Canadian Holy Mother with the girl's apotheosis on Holy Family Hill, pulling Jacques on a sled amid blue and gold sunset imagery.[50]

Interpretations by Woodress, Donovan, Rosowski, O'Brien, Skaggs, Fiddyment Levy, Roman, and other critics offer insights into Cather's vision of life and art and domestic order, and into the interplay of these forces in her fiction. Yet a study of *Shadows*, made in both the general context of her oeuvre and of the historical sources that informed the novel, reveals the work as even more pivotal in her career to that point than might at first be apparent. The work is particularly important in tracing Cather's growing need of order to make life potentially beautiful and significant, and in understanding how that artistic ordering could be explained in terms of a domesticity that encompasses diverse social classes and both secular and clerical forces. Through her fictionalized perspective of the history of New France, Cather can achieve in *Shadows* a sympathy between characters who remained at odds during their historical lives, and create from this fusion an impressionist portrait of the Auclairs' hearth. There, the proud strength of Quebec's most able civil potentate, Count Frontenac, and its first, most powerful bishop, François de Montmorency de Laval, could unite as integral parts of an innovative sociopolitical order based not on domesticity as an idyllic retreat, as it is often interpreted in *My Ántonia*, but as the cement of a Northeast community in which the private, familial order cannot exist separately from the larger political one.

This New World heroic also links individual achievement with the "communal and selfless"[51] literary artistry Jewett's example taught Cather to appreciate, and makes the communal world of women as healers and storytellers an equal force in a society politically governed by men. And the role of domesticity in Cather's equalizing and unifying New World creed continues to gain critical attention. Ann Romines, in *The Home Plot: Women, Writing and Domestic Ritual*, finds that, after her early works, which often appreciated domestic art more intellectually or aesthetically than viscerally, Cather refined and expanded her vision with her tale of Quebec. "In 1931, with *Shadows on the Rock*, Willa Cather finally made a full entry into the life of housekeeping as practiced by traditional women," Romines writes, "and such housekeeping became a central concern of the last, great decade of her writing life."[52] She adds, "In *Shadows on the Rock* and after, she sought ways to acknowledge and scrutinize the most deeply, ambivalently traditional women's plot: domestic ritual. And her fiction—as the thirties show—would never be the same."[53]

Cather's altered vision defines familial and societal energy in a way different from her earlier fiction, particularly a narrative viewed as exemplifying the same domestic themes as *Shadows*, *My Ántonia*. Critics have long viewed Ántonia Shimerda as the source of all energy in the work, a woman who, to Jim Burden, "had always been one to leave images in the mind that did not fade."[54] By extension, the energy and warmth of the novel come from the family that Ántonia's own life has created and not from larger political and religious spheres. In *Shadows*, by contrast, the work of an older writer, the central nuclear family is an incomplete one, centered around a pre-adolescent girl and her sensitive but ineffectual father, the apothecary Euclide Auclair. To an author who was also a member of a family facing illness and imminent death, this reassuring structure of a colony that was paradoxically new and traditional at once must have been particularly consoling. In its own way, *Shadows* may even have been more comforting for Cather than *Death Comes for the Archbishop* (1927), in that the later work offered physical and spiritual serenity for those living traditional lives, as members of an earthly as well as a celestial order, and not merely the detached calm of the "saint's legend" that critics like David Stouck have dubbed *Death Comes for the Archbishop*.[55]

In achieving the fusion of private and public order, Cather also created a New World standard by which even her beloved France fell short. As the humbled Bishop Saint-Vallier will tell an aged Auclair, "'You have done well to remain here where nothing changes'" (SOR, 277). From the perspective of Cather's new vision, the disruptions that have ruined France for the pioneers of Quebec are caused by a separation of order—private from public, political from domestic—that cannot occur in Cather's New France, with its larger idea of family as a social and political bond encompassing all orders. In interpreting her historical sources this way, Cather incorporates the fictional female communities of her mentor Sarah Orne Jewett but also goes beyond them in defying the separation of male and female realms by her conception of societal and familial order.[56] Capturing the special flavor of seventeenth-century New France, Cather enhances the symbolism of such a New World order by inset stories of Marian devotion and influence, to be discussed next, and further creates a new definition of the family that achieves a significance germane to French Canada. As Mme Pommier tells Cécile:

> "When we first came to this country, I was especially struck by the veneration in which the Holy Family was held in Kebec ... there is no other place in the world where the people are so devoted to the Holy Family as here in our own Canada. It is something very special to us." (SOR, 101)

Cather's use of this historical national devotion to bring together her growing love of New France and the Northeast, of an ever more elusive domestic center or family stability as a corollary and integer of public order, and of the simple wisdom she shared with Jewett, gave depth and beauty to her only novel set completely in this northern frontier. It also showed her affinity with the region that increasingly became a part of her art and life.

2

The Early Fiction, Its Connection to Cather's Life, and the Beginnings of *Shadows on the Rock*

When Cather published the first novel she claimed as her own, she dedicated it to Sarah Orne Jewett in words that expressed what she had gained from her mentor. "To the memory of SARAH ORNE JEWETT," Cather placed before the text of *O Pioneers!* (1913), "in whose beautiful and delicate work there is the perfection that endures." Yet in the earlier *Alexander's Bridge* (1912), despite Cather's later renunciation of the book, and in keeping with Merrill M. Skaggs's assertion that "there's a sense in which all Cather's convictions remained tentative . . . she often restlessly returned to the same starting point in order to set off in a new direction after an opposite conclusion,"[1] Jewett's influence is perhaps equally apparent; at the least, the imprint of Jewett's wisdom can be seen competing with the Jamesian touch that is often used to critically define *Alexander's Bridge.*

Domesticity, for example, especially as it is practiced by the rival women in Bartley Alexander's life, provides arguably the most genuine moments in a book that is easy to dismiss as derivative and stilted. It is, in Bartley's own words, the grace and intuitive charm of his wife Winifred that has "made his life, gratified his pride, given direction to his tastes and habits."[2] It is she who has filled his home with harmonious, beautiful things, including the hearth she tends and the flowers she expertly chooses and arranges, so that visiting professor Lucius Wilson can stand before the fire and say to his host's satisfaction, "'Bartley, if I'd had my choice of all possible places in which to spend Christmas, your house would certainly be the place I'd have chosen. Happy people do a great deal for their friends. A house like this throws its warmth out'" (AB, 64). It is precisely this domestic charm that most holds Bartley together, even in his terminal self-disintegration, as he considers with painful wonder: "How could this happen here, in his own house, among the things he loved?" (AB, 69).

Almost more than sexual magnetism, it is a similar homely charm that draws Bartley to Hilda Burgoyne. Cather's descriptive prose works to seduce the reader simultaneously with Bartley, as first Hilda's fidelity and vulnerability are revealed, and then her even more potent domestic simplicity. Both the reader and Bartley first observe and then appreciate the fine, simple things about her apartment, the bookcases and etchings and flowers, so that Bartley's words seem apt descriptions of her home. "'It's the air of the whole place here that I like. You haven't got anything that doesn't belong'" (AB, 50). The integrated elegance of Hilda's housekeeping is only enhanced and made more enduring by her pride as she guards her actress-mother's china and cups, themselves a legacy and wonder to Hilda herself as she muses,

> "Heaven knows how she managed to keep it whole, through all our wanderings, or in what baskets and bundles and theatre trunks it hasn't been stowed away. We always had our tea out of those blue cups when I was a little girl, sometimes in the queerest lodgings, and sometimes on a trunk at the theatre." (AB, 52)

Hilda's fidelity to her mother is no less striking than her constancy to Bartley Alexander, keeping her from ever marrying another. It is also part of a domestic harmony that is as strong in Hilda as, in her way, in Winifred, as both consoling and comforting women are contrasted with the volatile, destructive Bartley. Winifred's recognition of her husband's boundless and at times upsetting energy is gently humorous, as Alexander himself jokes to Lucius Wilson, after his attempts at arranging Christmas wreaths, "'I'll ring for Thomas to clear away this litter. Winifred says I always wreck the house when I try to do anything'" (AB, 64–65). For the more vulnerable Hilda, Bartley's inappropriateness around the house is more threatening, as she tells him, when he capriciously sends more flowers than she desires and offers her still other gifts for her home, "'No, there are some things you can't do'" (AB, 91).

Many other foretastes of Cather's more mature prose also inform *Alexander's Bridge* and belie her later rejections of the novel as not one of her own, including her early use of fire as a warm, revealing domestic touch, one that is present in such crucial scenes as Winifred's first meeting with Lucius Wilson and Hilda's closing conversation with him that serves as an epilogue to both Bartley's life and the book. Yet in other ways, Cather's assessment of the work as not in her most congenial style and tone seems correct, especially when placed against the more expansive and accomplished *O Pioneers!* The second novel, longer, more fully developed, and more uniquely Cather's own than *Alexander's Bridge*, owed even more to Jewett's influence. "I had the good fortune to meet Sarah Orne Jewett, who had read all of my early stories and had very clear and definite opinions about them and about where my work fell short," Cather said in an interview. "She said, 'Write it as it is, don't try to make it like this or that. You can't do it in anybody else's way—you will have to make a way of your own. If the way happens to be new, don't let that frighten you.'"[3]

Despite the often overlooked merits of *Alexander's Bridge* just described, *O Pioneers!* remains the more complete result of this fortunate meeting of two artists, and of the lessons Cather learned from Jewett.

> I dedicated my novel *O Pioneers!* to Miss Jewett because I had talked over some of the characters in it with her one day at Manchester, and in this book I tried to tell the story of the people as truthfully and simply as if I were telling it to her by word of mouth, Cather said.[4]

In seeking her own way by telling her own tale, as Jewett had encouraged her to do, Cather achieved what she would come to describe as the greatest artistic freedom she had known to that time. She wrote in the essay "My First Novels [There Were Two]":

> I began to write a book entirely for myself, a story about some Scandinavians and Bohemians who had been neighbours of ours when I lived on a ranch in Nebraska, when I was eight or nine

years old. I found it a much more absorbing occupation than writing *Alexander's Bridge*. . . . Here there was no arranging or "inventing"; everything was spontaneous and took its own place, right or wrong. This was like taking a ride through a familiar country on a horse that knew the way, on a fine morning when you felt like riding. . . . *O Pioneers!* interested me tremendously, because it had to do with a kind of country I loved, because it was about old neighbours, once very dear, whom I had almost forgotten in the hurry and excitement of growing up and finding out what the world was like and trying to get on in it.[5]

These words, as well as expressing Cather's own views of what makes enduring literature, also recall some of Jewett's best-known advice to her, to tell of things "which haunt the mind for years, and at last write themselves down."[6]

In considering Jewett's influence on Cather's career, critics have found that even *O Pioneers!* if not the earlier *Alexander's Bridge*, had predecessors like the story "The Enchanted Bluff" (1909) completed during Jewett's lifetime and geared to her tastes, as correspondence from Cather made plain. Cather described the story of six boys' reminiscences and dreams in a letter to Jewett as a story her friend might prefer to her earlier fiction because of Cather's use of her own materials, a Western setting, and characters.[7] It is a tale that is to Woodress a "rich evocation of her adolescence in Red Cloud" as well as a foreshadowing of her later major fiction, especially in its introduction of the legends of Coronado and the Spaniards on the Plains, in its use of a rock as a symbol of strength and escape, and in its mythical evocation of the Southwest.[8] A slightly later story, "The Bohemian Girl" (1912) though completed after Jewett's death, shows even more of Jewett's influence and moves directly toward the innovative *O Pioneers!* Virginia Faulkner, in editing Cather's collected stories, calls this work "quite different from any [Cather] had written in the past decade," and "the immediate precursor of *O Pioneers!*"[9]

The tale of an errant Nebraska boy, Nils Ericson, returned to reclaim the woman he loves from the stolid farm life that is killing her, "The Bohemian Girl" is laced with images of which a Mrs. Todd or Mrs. Blackett could be proud. Nils's and Clara's neglected love is first rekindled at the homey beer garden of Clara's father, Joe Vavrika, nestled "in a cheerfuller place, a little Bohemian settlement," with tables surrounded by "gooseberry bushes under his little cherry tree" (CSF, 21); it is here that Clara sits with her father of a Sunday afternoon, while the old man smokes "a long-tasseled porcelain pipe with a hunting scene painted on the bowl," with a "black cat . . . dozing in the sunlight at [Clara's] feet, and Joe's dachshund . . . scratching a hole under the scarlet geraniums and dreaming of badgers" (CSF, 24). An even more powerful domestic scene ultimately draws Clara and Nils together, the barn-raising supper that is the heart of the story and the clearest example of Cather's mastery of her natural material. It is after this supper that the two lovers are forced to confront their feelings, as Clara tries to sting Nils with the words, "'All the same, you don't really like gay people. . . . I could see that when you were looking at the old women there this afternoon. They're the kind you really admire, after all'" (CSF, 33). His actions belie these words, as Nils persuades Clara to leave with him, but for many readers it is precisely these rustic characters who breathe life into the story, despite the intended focus on Nils and Clara: the children romping in the haymow, for example, or Johanna Vavrika with her "platters heaped with fried chicken, her roasts of beef, boiled tongues, and baked hams with cloves stuck in the crisp brown fat and garnished with tansy and parsley"; or the "fine company of . . . fat, rosy old women who looked hot in their best dresses; spare, alert old women with brown, dark-veined hands; and several of almost heroic frame . . . all [of whom] had a pleased, prosperous air, as if they were more than satisfied with themselves and with life."[10]

As well as Cather's own accounts of the literary debt she owed Jewett, a consideration of her development in these early stories reveals the extent to which she valued Jewett's advice and approval. This early mentor/student relationship is also made apparent in Sharon O'Brien's comparison of the two artists' friendship and the one depicted in Jewett's "Martha's Lady." To O'Brien, the story is a "possible . . . intense response to [Cather's] . . . identification with Martha, the clumsy maid who learns housekeeping skills from Helena [Jewett]," with Helena serving as "both the model and the imagined audience for Martha's creativity—the reader of the texts she creates in table settings and flower arrangements."[11]

Cather's text in *O Pioneers!*, the work she dedicated to Jewett, is not a simple flower arrangement or table setting; yet in many respects the novel seems as true a tribute to Cather's mentor as Martha's domestic arranging is to Helena. In this first mature work, Cather at last followed her mentor's literary advice, to write of the things that have teased the mind for years, and in so doing she came far in her search for both her own voice and her spiritual center or home. She also succeeded in writing of an unusual, strong woman who, like Jewett's Mrs. Todd or Mrs. Blackett, becomes the center of her own world, so that Cather could conclude the novel with one of her greatest literary affirmations. "Fortunate country, that is one day to receive hearts like Alexandra's into its bosom, to give them out again in the yellow wheat, in the rustling corn, in the shining eyes of youth!"[12]

Alexandra is also significant in Cather's fiction as a transitional female hero, one midway between such complete domestic artists as Ántonia Shimerda and Cécile Auclair and the earlier Clara Vavrika Ericson or Winifred Alexander, who, because of the spareness of detail about her, is less satisfying as a fully developed character than as a symbol of Bartley Alexander's divided nature. Though she makes Alexandra more central to the story and a more rounded character than these earlier creations, Cather nonetheless uses broad strokes to paint the picture of the satisfying and rewarding home life Alexandra has achieved, in contrast to the warm, merged images of the family life of the Cuzaks', for example.

Alexandra's Divide, or fertile prairie land, is now tamed and friendly, "a vast checker-board, marked off in squares of wheat and corn," alive with "telephone wires [that] hum along white roads," "gayly painted farmhouses," and "gilded weathervanes on the big red barns [that] wink at each other across the green and brown and yellow fields" (OP, 75); it is now a land "thickly populated," with "something frank and joyous and young in the open face of the country" and an atmosphere ebullient with "the same tonic, puissant quality that is in the tilth, the same strength and resoluteness" (OP, 76–77). Alexandra is particularly at home in the broadly rendered Divide, in her large white house surrounded by

> so many sheds and outbuildings grouped about it that the place looked not unlike a tiny village. A stranger, approaching it, could not help noticing the beauty and fruitfulness of the outlying fields. There was something individual about the great farm, a most unusual trimness and care for detail. (OP, 83)

The house itself, by contrast, "is curiously unfinished and uneven in comfort ... [with] one room ... papered, carpeted, over-furnished; the next ... almost bare" (OP, 83–84). It is only outside of the house that

> you feel again the order and fine arrangement manifest all over the great farm; in the fencing and hedging, in the windbreaks and sheds, in the symmetrical pasture ponds ... [and] that, properly, Alexandra's house is the big out-of-doors, and that it is in the soil that she expresses herself best. (OP, 84)

Ántonia Shimerda Cuzak of *My Ántonia*, though in many ways as adept as Alexandra in designing the external farm, is more complete in being equally at home within the warmth of her own walls, and in bringing forth "a veritable explosion" of human life,[13] as well as Alexandra's "yellow wheat" and "rustling corn" (OP, 309). When Jim Burden at last returns, after nearly twenty years, Ántonia "pulled [her children] out of corners and came bringing them like a mother cat bringing in her kittens" for him to see and admire (MA, 332). She also has the same exuberance for all life on her farm, from the trees that she and Anton planted and watered by hand, and about which Ántonia says sympathetically, "'I love them as if they were people'" (MA, 340), to the drakes, "handsome fellows, with pinkish grey bodies, their heads and necks covered with iridescent green feathers which grew close and full, changing to blue like a peacock's neck" (MA, 341–42).

The result is a home that Cather, like Jim, can admire, a place more truly "a quiet centre of life" than any Cather had envisioned to that time. While he is there Jim enjoys the sensory impressions of "ducks and geese [that] ran quacking across my path" and white cats that "were sunning themselves among yellow pumpkins on the porch steps" (MA, 330); of Ántonia's full supper table, "two long rows of restless heads in the lamplight, and so many eyes fastened excitedly upon Án-tonia as she sat at the head of the table, filling the plates and starting the dishes on their way" (MA, 347); of Ántonia's fruit cellar with its barrels of pickles and preserved fruits, and her children as they reveal each treasure, tracing "on the glass with their finger-tips the outline of the cherries and strawber-ries and crabapples within, trying by a blissful expression of countenance to give . . . some idea of their deliciousness" (MA, 338); and of Ántonia's orchard, the center of "the deepest peace" for Jim on the entire farm, with its "crabs [that] hung on the branches as thick as beads on a string, purple-red, with a thin silvery glaze over them" (MA, 341).

Such impressions can only make Jim further acknowledge Ántonia's power, the unconscious artistry like that possessed by Jewett's finest characters, of being one always "to leave images in the mind that did not fade—that grew stronger with time" (MA, 352). These words, which Cather wrote to describe her best-known domestic artist, echo her earlier praise of an-other artist she treasured, Sarah Orne Jewett, in the previously cited dedication to *O Pioneers!* "To the memory of SARAH ORNE JEWETT in whose beautiful and delicate work there is the perfection that endures."

In later works, creating and holding the beautiful in life was an artistry that Cather's characters achieved with increas-ing difficulty. Claude Wheeler in *One of Ours* is so little at peace with his surroundings that, upon his death, his grieving mother can only reflect, "He died believing his own country better than it is, and France better than any country can ever be. . . . She would have dreaded the awakening,—she some-times even doubts whether he could have borne at all that last, desolating disappointment."[14] Marian Forrester, in *A Lost Lady* (1923), suffering from material losses and from having to witness the physical deterioration of the man she most ad-mired, her husband Captain Forrester, confesses that "'to me, it was as if one of the mountains had fallen down,'" and so becomes "like a ship without ballast, driven hither and thither by every wind."[15] Godfrey St-Peter of *The Professor's House* (1925) lives long enough to see his house so divided, physically and metaphorically, that he chooses to live much of his life in

isolation in an abandoned home, until he must face the ultimate question of whether to embrace life or death. And Myra
Henshawe, of *My Mortal Enemy* (1926), perhaps Cather's most
tortured creation, sees herself driven from one home to another. She is banished first from her uncle's "big stone house,
in its ten-acre park of trees" by her marriage to a man of whom
her uncle does not approve, and again from her fashionable
New York apartment with its "solidly built, high-ceiled rooms,
with snug fire-places and wide doors and deep windows"[16] because of her husband's poverty. Myra dies alone on a cliff overlooking the sea, near a "sprawling overgrown West-coast city"[17]
and granted a dubious forgiveness for her pride.

In *Death Comes for the Archbishop*, her work immediately
preceding *Shadows*, (1931), Cather turned to many of the
themes she would explore in her tale of French Canada and
wound together the threads of spiritual and domestic tranquillity and artistry as she had done in none of her novels since
My Ántonia. *Death Comes for the Archbishop* is like *Shadows* as
it unites domesticity, artistry, and the sacred around the central image of Mary as mother and, perhaps, as unconscious
woman-artist. Mary plays as key a role in *Death Comes for the
Archbishop* as in *Shadows* in creating an integrated social and
spiritual order in which the noblest and meanest members of
society are interdependent. Within this New World standard,
Fathers Latour and Vaillant are connected to those socially
below them through their devotion to Mary, forming a familial
world order with elements of the Christian matriarchy so
richly revealed in Sarah Orne Jewett's fiction. Cather, however,
moves beyond Jewett's simple matriarchy to an order that
transcends class and gender distinctions, and in which male
heroes are as capable of caring and practicing domestic arts
as are her strongest women.

Cather enriches the lives of her characters and enhances the
seemingly plotless narration of *Death Comes for the Archbishop*
with image-filled layers of meaning, layers made part of a symbolic whole by a common artistry and devotion traditionally
associated with women. On the simplest level, of the domesticity gleaned from centuries of civilized tradition to provide
meaning and order, Cather's Fathers Vaillant and Latour cling
with pride to their most basic customs. As Latour tells Father

Joseph, upon the latter's preparation of the traditional onion soup,

> Think of it, Blanchet; in all this vast country between the Mississippi and the Pacific Ocean, there is probably not another human being who could make a soup like this . . . a soup like this is not the work of one man. It is the result of a constantly refined tradition. There are nearly a thousand years of history in this soup.[18]

This emphasis on tradition, which will be echoed in Cécile Auclair's careful ministrations to her father, is again seen in Latour's insistence on tending gardens. Cather writes:

> Father Latour's recreation was his garden. He grew such fruit as was hardly to be found even in the old orchards of California; cherries and apricots, apples and quinces, and the peerless pears of France—even the most delicate varieties. He urged the new priests to plant fruit trees wherever they went, and to encourage the Mexicans to add fruit to their starchy diet. Wherever there was a French priest, there should be a garden of fruit trees and vegetables and flowers. He often quoted to his students that passage from their fellow Auvergnat, Pascal: that Man was lost and saved in a garden. (DCA, 267)

Earlier in the novel Cather further elevates the traditional domesticity of Latour's gardening by implicitly comparing his earthly yield to the fruits of his religious endeavors. Latour's garden, she writes,

> had been laid out six years ago, when the Bishop brought his fruit trees . . . up from St. Louis in wagons, along with the blessed Sisters of Loretto, who came to found the Academy of Our Lady of Light. The school was now well established, reckoned a benefit to the community by Protestants as well as Catholics, and the trees were bearing. Cuttings from them were already yielding fruit in many Mexican gardens. (DCA, 201)

In these sentences, Cather joins domesticity and religious vocation under a Marian influence, to bear fruit in the presence of Our Lady of Light.

Moving beyond an earthly domesticity which leads to spirituality, Cather lifts Marian devotion to both human palpability and to the highest level of artistry. Facing the prospect of separation from his lifelong friend Father Joseph, and indulging in such "reflections as any bachelor nearing fifty might have," Latour compares his own missionary loneliness to the life he could have had as a parish priest in his native France, surrounded by "nephews coming to him for help in their Latin or a bit of pocket-money; nieces to run into his garden and bring their sewing and keep an eye on his housekeeping" (DCA, 255). Though he has sacrificed this, what Latour learns he does possess, upon returning home and entering his study, is "not a solitude of atrophy, of negation, but of perpetual flowering," warmed by "the sense of a Presence awaiting him." This presence, in the physical manifestation of a small wooden statue of Mary, is the recognition that "a life need not be cold, or devoid of grace in the worldly sense, if it were filled by Her who was all the graces; Virgin-daughter, Virgin-mother, girl of the people and Queen of Heaven: le rêve suprême de la chair" (DCA, 256).

This same Mary, more than human in her warmth and compassion, is also supernatural in what her earthly incarnation, the wooden statue, symbolizes, both to Latour and to his uneducated parishioners, and in her power to bring the worldly prelate and his humble parishioners together. "The women loved to sew for her and the silversmiths to make her chains and brooches," Latour reflects. He "had delighted her wardrobe keepers when he told them he did not believe the Queen of England or the Empress of France had so many costumes. She was their doll and their queen, something to fondle and something to adore, as Mary's Son must have been to Her" (DCA, 256–57). Latour further removes Mary into the realms of art and of supreme spirituality by remarking,

These poor Mexicans . . . were not the first to pour out their love in this simple fashion. Raphael and Titian had made costumes for Her in their time, and the great masters had made music for Her, and the great architects had built cathedrals for Her. Long before Her years on earth, in the long twilight between the Fall and the Redemption, the pagan sculptors were always trying to achieve the image of a goddess who should yet be a woman. (DCA, 257)

More than in individual scenes even as powerfully concise as these, Cather advanced her search for meaning through inset stories of Marianism like those she would employ in *Shadows*. These stories comfort and connect her characters, human sufferers more united by the solace they find in a common mother than they are separated by differences in their earthly stations. Such inset stories, far from being incidental, also advance the overall development of Cather's narration. Chapters 1 and 2 of book 7, "The Great Diocese," for example, taken together, form the spiritual center of *Death Comes for the Archbishop*. In chapter 1, "The Month of May," Father Vaillant finds a revitalization of his faith and a sense of direction for the rest of his life, through the power of Mary, as does Father Latour in chapter 2, "December Night."

For Father Vaillant, convalescing with the bishop from malaria, "It was the month of Mary and the month of May" (DCA, 200), the month of the year he had selected from "his boyhood . . . to be the holy month of the year for him, dedicated to the contemplation of his Gracious Patroness" (DCA, 202). As a reward for this devotion, Vaillant believes that "ever since then, all the most important events in his own history had occurred in the blessed month when this sinful and sullied world puts on white as if to commemorate the Annunciation, and becomes, for a little, lovely enough to be in truth the Bride of Christ" (DCA, 204). During this particular May, freed from his missionary's chores by his illness,

> the month of Mary he had been able to give to Mary; to Her he had consecrated his waking hours. At night he sank to sleep with the sense of Her protection. In the morning when he awoke, before he had opened his eyes, he was conscious of a special sweetness in the air,—Mary, and the month of May. Alma Mater redemptoris! Once more he had been able to worship with the ardour of a young religious, for whom religion is pure personal devotion, unalloyed by expediency and the benumbing cares of a missionary's work. (DCA, 203)

The result of Vaillant's regeneration is his renewed missionary work near Tucson and the desire to find "the faith, in that wild frontier, [that] is like a buried treasure," the recovery of which "will be the greatest happiness of my life" (DCA, 207).

More isolated in a human sense than ever by granting his friend's request to leave, Latour, in the connecting chapter,

"December Night," must also face his own dark night of the soul. For Latour, as for Vaillant, the power of Mary and of his parishioners' belief in her is also the power that saves. Cather reinforces the power of Mary's healing, maternal artistry by providing relief for Latour's spiritual barrenness in the child-like devotion and simplicity of the old slave Sada. Driven into his own church by "the coldness and doubt . . . [that] made him feel an alien, wherever he was," Latour is greeted by Sada and by the Marian devotion that makes her fall on her knees and kiss "the feet of the Holy Mother, the pedestal [in the Lady Chapel] on which they stood, crying all the while . . . . 'Oh Holy Mary, Queen of Virgins. . . .'" (DCA, 214). Latour gives Sada a physical manifestation of their common faith, a thin silver medal of Mary, but she gives him something far greater: the actual possession of faith and not its mere physical representation.

In this scene, Cather brings into sharper focus Mary's power to unite the suffering members of her family, however dispa-rate their social positions, as Latour gets to know Mary in a more personal sense as his mother than has ever been granted him. Cather writes:

> He seemed able to feel all it meant to her [Sada] to know that there was a Kind Woman in Heaven, though there were such cruel ones on earth. Old people, who have felt blows and toil and known the world's hard hand, need, even more than children do, a woman's tenderness. Only a Woman, divine, could know all that a woman can suffer. Not often, indeed, had Jean Marie Latour come so near to the Fountain of all Pity . . . the pity that no man born of woman could ever utterly cut himself off from. . . . The beautiful concept of Mary pierced the priest's heart like a sword. (DCA, 217–18)

The image of Mary as mother and hope is completed when Latour feels with Sada "how that name [Mary] was food and raiment, friend and mother" (DCA, 218), and his world is no longer barren, but instead "the peace without seemed all one with the peace in his own soul" (DCA, 219). This peace is only attained after Latour recognizes his own place in the larger communal order.

Latour's humility, of becoming one with the humblest of his

parishioners, foreshadows the pioneering vision Cather explored even more centrally in *Shadows*. Her selection and handling of characters and themes in *Death Comes for the Archbishop* look back to serenity as elusive in the years between the world wars as it is reminiscent of the peacefulness of Mrs. Todd's rural Maine, as they look ahead to her next novel in which communal religious and domestic traditions give life meaning, *Shadows*. In *Shadows*, her differing fictional treatments of two of the best-known female religious of New France underscore the importance the aging artist placed upon membership in a larger family order, one in which public and private belonging were interrelated and vital. Such a union also relates Jewett's vision of a healing community to the integrating Marian devotion Cather saw as essential to the permanence and stability of *Shadows*.

That Cather found such comfort and belonging attractive in the late 1920s, when she began writing the novel, is understandable. During this time she suffered a forced move from her apartment at Number 5, Bank Street, and the subsequent, unsettling relocation to the Grosvenor Hotel. Her sorrows intensified in the years to come, culminating with the death of her father, Charles Cather, in March of 1928, and her mother's stroke in December of the same year. The writing of *Shadows* was frequently interrupted by trips to California to visit her ailing mother, and the work on the novel which suggested itself to her almost by chance became, according to Edith Lewis, "a great release" from her cares.[19]

The discovery of Quebec in the summer of 1928, while en route to Grand Manan,[20] was fortunate for Cather. Not only did this voyage provide her with a subject for a new novel, and so help her fill the emptiness she was feeling after the completion of *Death Comes for the Archbishop*, but it also allowed her to explore further, and again become a part of, the healing and forgiving world of the earlier novel. While attempting to make the best of her enforced first stay in Quebec, prolonged by Edith Lewis's attack of influenza, Cather discovered the city alone, reveling, Lewis tells us, in "its extraordinary French character, isolated and kept intact through hundreds of years, as if by a miracle, on this great un-French continent."[21] According to Lewis, among the books of Canadian history Cather encountered during this stay were Francis Park-man's histories of Canada, Abbé Henri Scott's biography of Bishop Laval, the *Jesuit Relations*, La Hontan's *Voyages*, and the *Memoirs* of Saint-Simon.[22] Other critics cite additional works Cather read in preparation for her writing, including Leblond de Brumath's biography of Laval and accounts of the life of Mère Catherine de Saint-Augustin by Mère Juschereau of the Hôtel Dieu and by Catherine's confessor and advisor, Father Paul Ragueneau.[23] For her depictions of the recluse Jeanne Le Ber, Cather probably turned to Parkman's compendious histories,[24] although more detailed accounts of Le Ber existed, most notably Étienne Faillon's 1861 biography.

Cather may have turned to Faillon's sacred account of Le Ber, as she consulted church sources on Laval and Catherine de Saint-Augustin, to balance Parkman's bias against the Roman faith, especially as manifested in North America. Of the ultimate failure of the Jesuits and their beliefs in Canada, Parkman wrote:

> The contest on this continent between Liberty [English Protestant-ism] and Absolutism [French Catholicism] was never doubtful. . . . Populations formed in the ideas and habits of a feudal monarchy, and controlled by a hierarchy profoundly hostile to freedom of thought, would have remained a hindrance and a stumbling-block in the way of that majestic experiment of which America is the field.[25]

He states his case even more strongly, and damns not only the Jesuits or the clergy, in *Count Frontenac and New France Under Louis XIV.*

> Whence came the numerical weakness of New France, and the real though latent strength of her rivals? . . . As soon could the Ethiopian change his skin as the priest-ridden King change his fatal policy of exclusion [of the persecuted protestant Huguenots from emigrating to New France]. Canada must be bound to the papacy, even if it blasted her. The contest for the west must be waged by the means which Bourbon policy ordained, and which, it must be admitted, had some great advantages of their own when controlled by a man like Frontenac.[26]

Parkman makes it quite obvious that all rulers were not as able as Frontenac, and that the fate of a people benighted by fedualism and "blasted" by subservience to the Pope was sealed years before Quebec fell to the English.[27] Yet even amid his sweeping likes and antipathies, the anti-Roman historian at times writes with an ambiguity that Cather seems to reflect in her fiction, especially in his almost begrudging praise of certain characteristics of the Jesuits and in his open admiration for New France's greatest civil leader, a man who nearly achieves greatness in Parkman's eyes despite being an agent of the flawed Bourbon policy. As will be discussed in the following section, in his treatment of Laval Parkman can admit a humble devotion in the domineering patriarch's demeanor before the Virgin Mother, and he can praise the "marvels" and "miracles of patient suffering and daring enterprise" of other Jesuits as they worked among their Indian converts.[28] And when he turned away from the clerics to Frontenac, Parkman comes as close as he can to praising the feudalistic system he sees as ultimately doomed. These are the subtexts to which Cather was sensitive in her reading of Parkman, and to which she added her own intuitions as well as divergent accounts of biographers and historians more friendly to Catholicism in creating her own characters and in telling her own tale.

To illuminate the role of the larger public and sacred orders in Cather's search for integration, and to help understand the central roles of Laval and Frontenac in her New World vision, an analysis of Cather's differing adaptations of the histories of two more minor if equally symbolic characters merits consideration. Both Jeanne Le Ber, the recluse of "Ville Marie" or Montreal, and Mère Catherine de Saint-Augustin of Quebec's Hôpital Dieu were known for their extraordinary piety. Both women, of noble families and lineage, also rejected high worldly estates for their religious callings. And both defied parents and families to renounce the world in favor of the service of Christ. Historically and in Cather's fiction, however, Jeanne Le Ber led the more isolated life, choosing not even to join a religious order but rather to have herself virtually walled into a stone cell in the Sisters of the Congregation Church, rejecting father, mother, and all suitors for solitude and, as Cather and Le Ber's biographer Étienne Faillon make clear, a life of spiritual and personal aridity.

Catherine de Saint-Augustin, on the other hand, though as

spiritually tormented as Jeanne Le Ber, did function in and of the world, working in the hospital with the sick and with her order's own novices, and maintaining loving bonds with family and her religious community as long as she lived. And although her biographer and confessor, Father Paul Ragueneau, later revealed Catherine's demonic tortures and temptations, he only praised them as greater proof of her piety. Instead of adopting Ragueneau's interpretation, Cather chose to disregard the darker aspects of Mother Catherine's life and to focus on the young woman's virtue, communal service, and devotion to Mary. Mother Catherine, unlike the isolate Jeanne Le Ber, thus became suitable historical material for Cather's own fictive transmutation, revealing the need Cather felt and the importance she placed on domestic tranquillity and its power to connect the individual with eternal forces and traditions.

In *Shadows*, Cather describes Jeanne Le Ber, first through Cécile and Blinker's more credulous eyes, as a recluse whose miraculous life and uncommon sacrifices "brought pleasure, as if the recluse herself had sent to all those families whom she did not know some living beauty . . . an incomparable gift. In the long evenings . . . someone would speak the name of Jeanne Le Ber, and it again gave out fragrance." Her gift of faith is "the actual flowering of desire . . . [in which] the vague worship and devotion of the simple-hearted assumes a form."[29] Le Ber's cultural legacy is a real one in the novel, and critics like Ann Romines accept Cécile's view, seeing such isolates as "pardoxically giv[ing] themselves to the very communities they left" and becoming "their own mysterious legends, which nourish and sustain the villagers who perpetuate them."[30] Hermione Lee, in *Willa Cather—Double Lives*, also interprets Cécile and Blinker's view of the recluse as Le Ber turns "herself into a legend which provides lasting and beautiful images out of her private language," though she undercuts Le Ber's actions as "the paradox of legends . . . [in which] consolatory, educative life stories come out of personal suffering." Lee goes on to describe this suffering as great enough finally to render Le Ber's story one that "is not suitable for children."[31]

Despite her initial positive depictions of the recluse's life, ostensibly told through the veil of Cécile's approving memory, Cather also chooses words to describe Le Ber that subtly undercut Cécile and Blinker's interpretation. She describes how Le Ber's parent's "hearts grew heavier" (SOR, 132) at their prized daughter's unnatural sacrifice, and how, completely against the spirit of filial sentiment Edith Lewis and others tell us Cather was herself feeling at the time she was writing *Shadows*, Jeanne rejected all family connection, so that from the day "she took her vow, they [her parents and siblings] never had speech with her or saw her face,—never saw her bodily form . . . [and her father] avoided the house that had become the tomb of his hopes" (SOR, 133). Even more unnaturally, Jeanne refused to go to her mother's deathbed but instead only sent the message through a servant, "'Tell her I am praying for her, night and day'" (SOR, 133). Cather goes on to speak of "Jeanne's entombment and her cell" on the following page, foreshadowing, even in a child's positive view of Le Ber, the darker perspective on the recluse's actions she later reveals through Pierre Charron's eyes.

In Le Ber's alienation from humanity—and, Charron fears, from God—the woodsman interprets as tantamount to death the recluse's abandoning of the human bond that is the greatest comfort the lonely colony has to offer. "'Now she is no better than dead. Worse'" (SOR, 178), Charron tells Euclide Auclair, and again, "'one does not love a woman who has been dead for nearly twenty years'" (SOR, 181). Cather further undermines the more credulous Cécile's account of Le Ber through Charron's description of the woman he espied one cold winter night in her church-prison, a woman with a face that "was like a stone face; it had been through every sorrow.'" Charron, sensing no fragrance or joy of miracle in the recluse's life, describes her as speaking with a voice "hoarse, hollow, with the sound of despair in it . . . such resignation and despair! It froze everything in me'" (SOR, 183).

Historical accounts, even intentionally laudatory ones, of Jeanne Le Ber, relate many of the same facts as Charron's narration, making the recluse's life seem particularly appalling to an artist who was also a daughter facing the imminent loss of her remaining parent. In his *Christian Heroine of Canada; or, Life of Miss Le Ber*, an obscure work which Cather may have known primarily in outline from Parkman's condensed borrowing, Étienne Faillon tells of Le Ber's "heroic conduct"[32] at the time of her mother's death. Then in her first seclusion, under a vow of silence and solitude within her parent's house, Le Ber, despite a "secret anguish . . . when her dying mother's sobs reached her cell," remained in her room praying, "knowing that she could in no-wise alleviate these sufferings which she so keenly felt. . . . She did not even quit her cell, to bestow the last proofs of filial love, on her dying parent."[33] In even more powerful images, Faillon describes Le Ber as only quitting her cell after her mother's death and "modestly approaching the bed of death" where she "bends her knees in prayer, presses to her lips the hand of her departed mother, and bathes it with her tears."[34] Faillon similarly praises Le Ber for declining her widowed father's request to leave her reclusion and help him in the raising of his remaining "three sons younger than our heroine."[35] The historian equally honors Le Ber's behavior at her father's death, many years later, when "she testified her love by praying for him," never asking "to quit her cell in order to console him when he lay on his death bed," and refusing even to attend his funeral, conducted in the very church in which she was by then entombed in a stone cell behind the altar, though "she must needs have heard the sorrowful chants that accompany such ceremonies."[36]

Cather's fiction parallels Le Ber's life in another important aspect, the aridity of the recluse's last years just described by Charron as "resignation and despair" (SOR, 183). For the recluse's biographer, the spiritual emptiness that settled upon her was merely a final trial, and one that led to her even greater triumph for persevering in her solitary life. As Faillon writes:

God was pleased to treat sister Le Ber as He does heroic souls and to teach her solid virtue which is founded on interior abnegation. He deprived her of the celestial light which had illumined her soul for many years, and withdrew those ineffable consolations which had previously drawn her towards Him, and had often seemed to give her wings to reach the throne of God. . . . When the Almighty withdrew these favours from Sister Le Ber, her hours of meditation became hours of severe trial: her mind seemed darkened, and her heart cold and callous. . . . Thus it was she spent the last twenty years of her life; and these trials tended to strengthen her virtue.[37]

In Charron's anguished words, Cather echoes Faillon and intensifies Le Ber's loss, so that the final image she creates of Le Ber is a bleakly ambiguous portrait of a soul tormented and cut off from both worldly and spiritual domestic pleasures. In this respect Le Ber can be compared to other characters in Cather's fiction, from Thea Kronborg, who also does not return to her mother's deathbed but who has the satisfaction of her own artistry to sustain her, to Lucy Gayheart, who rejects an early mentor's advice to seek the pleasures of family and home and so perishes with neither Kronborg's artistic fruition nor with Ántonia Shimerda Cuzak's fecundity.

Even within *Shadows*, Cather uses historical sources not unlike the actual life of Le Ber to create a foil for the heart-emptiness of the recluse. Biographers of Mother Catherine de Saint-Augustin show a religious nearly as physically and spiritually troubled as Jeanne Le Ber. Cather's Mother Catherine, by contrast, is more completely a creature of light than such biographers suggest. In *Shadows* she braves the stormy Atlantic waves in a fragile wooden ship at the age of sixteen to come and serve Canada, prays souls suffering in purgatory into heaven, and unremittingly serves both God and her fellow creatures at the Hôpital Dieu. Cather even more clearly differentiates Catherine from the recluse Le Ber by depicting the link Catherine maintained with her order and with her faith, even in her times of greatest torment. The connection and communal belonging humanize Mother Catherine and render her a more completely positive symbol in the novel, even as Le Ber's lack of bonding dehumanizes her and enhances her painful isolation.

The historical Mother Catherine, like the actual Jeanne Le Ber, chose a religious life at an early age, and against her fond and cultured parents' wishes. Catherine's biographer, the Reverend Paul Ragueneau, in the account Cather most likely read, explains Catherine's father's change of heart in these words:

> [Shortly after Catherine redoubled her prayers to heaven], the heart of Monsieur du Longpré [Catherine's father] was happily changed: Our Lord having willed that this good man fall ill of chagrin and melancholy, Monsieur du Longpré asked to see a [*Jesuit*] *Relation* newly sent from Canada, which spoke of the death of Father Isaac Jogues, massacred by the Iroquois the year before,

1647, when he had gone for the third time to their country, to carry the faith of Jesus Christ to them. Assailed by sadness and a sudden drowsiness, Monsieur du Longpré succumbed to sleep, doubtless of a mysterious origin, during which he was inspired and convinced to allow our Catherine to make this great journey; and Catherine's mother had the same thought at the same time, although she was not with her husband. Upon awakening, his feelings were entirely changed regarding this generous sacrifice his daughter wished to make; and he conceived such a lively apprehension that God would demand payment at the hour of his death for his obstinant opposition to His will and to heaven's designs for his daughter, that, seized by this thought that held him fast, he accorded to God what he had refused to men.[38] (translation mine)

While retaining the historical outcome of Monsieur du Longpré's struggle, Cather altered Ragueneau's narrative so that the father's conversion had more to do with Catherine's insistence than with divine intercession. To Cather, the child's difference with her parents was resolved only after her incessant pleading to take orders and go to Canada came to the attention of the queen mother, Anne of Austria. "The Queen's intercession won her father's consent" (SOR, 41), Cather writes in contrast to Ragueneau's addition of personal spiritual revelation to the queen mother's request.

Despite these differences, in both Cather's and Ragueneau's accounts the grieving Monsieur du Longpré willingly changed his mind and gave his daughter up to a higher good and to a nobler home, to an order created to work for and with the poor, unlike the unreconciled Jacques Le Ber who grieved for his daughter to his death and lived to see her not loved by others as part of a larger family, but entombed in spiritual and physical desolation. Cather also reflects the admiration and affection Catherine's biographers report from all who knew her, from her loving family to the first order she entered at Bayeux, where, according to Ragueneau,

she was loved by all who knew her and whom she was leaving . . . the religious community at Bayeux where she had two sisters, her grandmother, a great aunt, and a first cousin, the founder of the House, and where all the other religious carried her in their hearts, and for whom she had limitless tenderness—separation from all this dear community caused her a sadness more painful than she could express.[39] (translation mine)

Cather's Mother Catherine is similarly venerated by all who know her, including Mother Juschereau who tells her tale in *Shadows* and recalls personal love for her many years after her death. "'When you speak her name,'" Cather's usually efficient and practical Mother Juschereau admits to an importuning Cécile, "'the stories come'" (SOR, 37). This is an uncharacteristic wistfulness for Cather's "hardy, sagacious, practical" (SOR, 42) Juschereau, but it is also the kind of response Catherine's name, to her biographer as well as to Cather, elicits.

Such a comparison of Ragueneau's and of Cather's Mother Catherine reveals that in the historical religious Cather found an apt antecedent for her representation of domestic unity. Cather's mutings of some of Ragueneau's details, however, make her Catherine de Saint-Augustin an even more powerful symbol of a life lived unstintingly for and with others, and for the good of a family order that transcended blood ties. She also becomes more than ever antithetical to Le Ber, who, with an even greater sacrifice, achieves a symbolic connection with those around her, but no human one, and so remains a more darkly ambiguous part of the communal legacy of New France.

In this depiction of Catherine, Cather wove many other historical strands of the woman's life into fiction, all of them working to humanize the young religious and to make her less isolated than the recluse Jeanne Le Ber. These biographical borrowings include Catherine's spiritual guidance by the martyred Jesuit Father Brébeuf and her closeness to Mary. This Marian devotion, unlike Le Ber's solitary prayers, also worked to bring Catherine closer to others and to promote their good. One of the most striking anecdotes in *Shadows*, for example, concerns the old sinner Marie who died abandoned in France, only to be prayed to salvation in Canada through the mercy of Mary and the efforts of Mother Catherine. Dying alone like "some unclean animal" (SOR, 37), Marie is so thoroughly considered lost that even Catherine offers no prayers for her soul until Marie appears and begs her prayers, telling the young religious how she was saved from hell through a deathbed prayer to Mary, who also abridged her stay in purgatory and bid her ask Catherine for a few masses to complete her penance. The deathbed prayer Cather attributes to Marie is as follows: "Queen of Heaven, you are the last refuge of the ruined and the outcast; I am abandoned by all the world; I have no hope but you; you alone have power to reach where I am fallen; Mary, Mother of Jesus, have pity upon me!" (SOR, 38).

Cather's narration of Marie's life, death, and salvation is strikingly like the historical one given by Paul Ragueneau, from their common account of Marie appearing to Catherine exactly twelve years after her death in France, with a sentence in purgatory abbreviated by Mary, to the dying prayer historically attributed to Marie for the salvation of her soul. "Alas! Holy Virgin Mary, I am not worthy to bear your name; but I pray you suffer not that I be damned. I give thanks to you for this name."[40] (translation mine) In both the fictional and the ostensibly factual accounts Marie is saved, but not until she has been cleansed of sin and its punishment, an isolation from a community as Mother Catherine has never been isolated, and an even more severe spiritual separation "from God, the Holy Virgin, the Saints ... [and] the sacraments"[41] (translation mine), according to Ragueneau, a fate from which Cather also saves her Catherine de Saint-Augustin.

In a more indirect borrowing from historical sources, and to create a sharper antithesis between the communal Mother Catherine and the equally tormented but isolated Jeanne Le Ber, Cather relates the connection between Catherine and the martyred Jesuit Father Brébeuf in a far less ambiguous light than does Catherine's biographer. The religious depicted in Ragueneu's *Vie de la Mère Catherine de Saint-Augustin* is clearly heroic to her biographer, but the priest's exploration of the forces against which the young nun needed sustaining, seems alien to secular, twentieth-century readers. Ragueneau writes:

God often allowed her to become like a prison to several thousand demons, who found themselves compelled, despite all their resistance, to enter this truly holy girl, of whom they had greater horror than of hell itself: Because no matter how they vented their rage against her, by subjecting her to all sorts of extreme and vivid temptations, these evil spirits from hell always were vanquished by this soul who was so faithful to the grace of Jesus Christ, that never could they gain her consent to the least thing they desired. ... So that so far from possessing her, they were themselves captives in her; and could do no more against others than against her; and often the number of temptations was so great and overwhelming, that this poor young girl felt as if she were combatting entire armies of demons.[42] (translation mine)

In these historical accounts, Father Brébeuf first came to Catherine through God's mercy, to aid her against these temptations and assaults. As Ragueneau explains,

> It was to this great servant of God, this great apostolic man, first Apostle to the Hurons, that Jesus Christ confided the care of his faithful servant and wife [Mother Catherine], in order to safeguard her against all the attacks and surprises from the demons, and to be for her spiritual director, in the very difficult and dangerous path along which divine Providence wanted to lead her to great sanctity.[43] (translation mine)

Such passages stand in strong contrast to Cather's account of Catherine's relationship with Father Brébeuf. In *Shadows,* the martyred priest appears to Catherine to tell "her of the glories of heaven, and . . . [give] her counsel and advice for all her perplexities in this world." Cather's "hero priest from paradise" comes to sustain the "slight, nervous, sickly" young religious as she endures a life of "vigils, mortifications, visions, raptures . . . [and] a steady routine of manual labour and administrative work, [while] observing the full discipline of her order" (SOR, 42).

Ragueneau records numerous examples of Catherine's temptations and of Brébeuf's guidance, in accounts Cather read both in *La Vie* and in Mother Juschereau's *Annals de l'Hôtel Dieu de Québec.* In her fiction, however, Cather omits all of the references just cited and instead invents Brébeuf as he helps the dying Mother Catherine to select Jeanne Franc Juschereau de la Ferté to be her successor as superior of the Hôtel Dieu. In fact, Mother Catherine never attained the post of mother superior of the order, but of director of the hospital and its novices, and although Juschereau was indeed a strong leader of her order, serving as mother superior for twenty-four years, her first election to that office did not occur until 1673, five years after Mother Catherine's death.[44]

In considering Cather's astute knowledge of history, it is unlikely that she was unaware of the liberties she was taking with historical accounts. To tell her story of New France in the time of Count Frontenac, she simply selected details to create the most realistically positive images possible of Mother Catherine. The sainted nun then could better serve as a model of Marian devotion and of religious domesticity not only for a naive Cécile, but also for the more skeptical, adult citizens of New France, and so help make Quebec an even more believable and deserving spiritual center. In such a world, beauty and fulfillment were attainable only by belonging to a collective private and public order. With Cécile as the focus of her novel, and with the elevation of the child to the status of Cather's ultimate domestic artist, *Shadows* became the embodiment of the New World heroic in which Cather, at midlife, came to place her trust.

3

Shadows on the Rock and Cather's Interpretation of the History of New France

At the heart of *Shadows on the Rock* is the security of Cécile wrapped within "layers and layers of shelter," of "the great grey river choked with ice and frozen snow, the never-ending, merciless forest beyond"; of the "dripping grey roofs and spires, the lighted windows among the crooked streets" of Quebec; and finally of "this one flickering, shadowy room at the core" in which she rests warm and secure.[1] Cécile's domestic center, in short, is Cather's representation of the security of home, of what, during her most trying years to that time, became the "quiet centre" of her life.

The immutability of Quebec is reinforced in *Shadows* by the count's strong arm behind Cécile and Euclide, by the spiritual and temporal protection of the church, symbolized by Bishop Laval and to lesser degrees by Jeanne Le Ber and Mother Catherine de Saint-Augustin, and by Pierre Charron's dash and daring, yet enduring vitality, that comes to symbolize the greatest authority for Cécile. Surrounded by these forces, Cécile can make "the days,—the complexion, the special flavour, the special happiness of each day as it passed . . . life itself" (SOR, 198); Cather, too, by conceiving Cécile, creates her own domestic center, one not unlike the home of Jewett's Mrs. Blackett on Green Island, that comforting room with its worn Bible, glasses, thimble, and sewing, in which lived "that heart which had made the most of everything that needed love!"[2] In developing her fictional characters from their historical antecedents and selecting details with which to embellish their lives, Cather revealed how the artist's vision scanned the pages of turbulent history and came to rest upon Quebec as the emblem of stability, tradition, and peace.

Cementing the new familial order of this center was the paternal strength of Laval and Frontenac, ameliorated by the influences of Mary and exemplified in the daily life of Quebec in the Auclair family and in its dependents. In creating such a new standard, what Hermione Lee describes as "the point where inherited European traditions were adapting to the challenge of New World conditions,"[3] Cather merged conventional maternal and paternal symbols to create the Canadian frontier of her fiction. She also defined all of her characters, even the most traditionally virile or patriarchal, by traits essential to such a frontier, especially a respect for home and family that makes all human life in New France part of a "sanctified family".[4]

Cather's Bishop François de Montmorency de Laval, for instance, is a far more amiable, fatherly figure than the one presented by her source, Francis Parkman. Parkman condemns Laval and all of the Jesuits of New France for their spiritual oppression of the colonists and for their hunger for power, writing, "Foremost among the envoys of the [Roman Catholic] faith were the members of that mighty order, who, in another hemisphere, had already done so much to turn back the advancing tide of religious freedom, and strengthen the arm of Rome."[5] He damns Laval in particular for his worldly aspirations, saying, "He believed firmly that the princes and rulers of this world ought to be subject to guidance and control at the hands of the Pope, Vicar of Christ on earth," with Laval as the Vicar's vicar in Canada; and that,

> of the faults which he owed to nature, the principal seems to have been an arbitrary and domineering temper . . . humility was the virtue to the culture of which he gave his chief attention, but soil and climate were not favorable. . . . In his stubborn fight for ecclesiastical ascendancy, he was aided by the impulses of a nature that loved to rule, and could not endure to yield.[6]

Parkman goes further in his *Count Frontenac and New France Under Louis XIV*, quoting Frontenac, before his recall as governor largely at Laval's insistence, as saying, "'Nearly all the disorders in New France spring from the ambition of the ecclesiastics, who want to join to their spiritual authority an absolute power over things temporal, and who persecute all who do not submit entirely to them.'"[7]

Parkman also interprets Laval's many documented sacrifices for his flock in a self-serving light. "Austerities and mortifications, playing at beggar, sleeping in beds full of fleas, or performing prodigies of gratuitous dirtiness in hospitals, however fatal to self-respect, could avail little against . . . the most subtle of human vices [pride],"[8] he writes, thus suggesting no similarity between his subject and the bishop Cather so lovingly portrayed, despite the fact that Cather followed the historical chronology of the prelate's life set forth by Parkman and borrowed her physical description of the great cleric directly from him.

Parkman's and Cather's physical depictions of Laval are very similar, though Cather's selection of details even in this matter does much to reveal the character she wished to create in the Quebec of her fiction. In *Count Frontenac* Parkman introduced Bishop Laval into his Canadian history as a man whose striking physical appearance announces a character formed by a drive for power. "A drooping nose of portentous size," Parkman writes; "a well-formed forehead; a brow strongly arched; a bright, clear eye; scanty hair, half hidden by a black skullcap; thin lips, compressed and rigid, betraying a spirit not easy to move or convince . . . such is Laval, as he looks grimly down on us from the dingy canvas of two centuries ago."[9] Cather borrowed her physical description of the renowned cleric directly from Parkman's portrait. Like his, her Laval, especially as presented in book 2 of *Shadows*, talking to Cécile and Jacques in Quebec's Notre Dame de la Victoire Church, is

> a very heavy, tall old man with wide, stooping shoulders and a head hanging forward . . . [wearing a] shovel hat and . . . a black skull-cap over his scanty locks. . . . His eyes were large and full, but set deep back under his forehead. He had such a very large, drooping nose, and such a grim, bitter mouth, that he might well have frightened a child who didn't know him. (SOR, 68–69)

Even as she retained the physical description she had inherited, however, Cather humanized Laval. Extending his character beyond that of a power-wielding patriarch battling with governors-general and politicking at the council of Quebec, Cather presents him in a range of situations, alone in silent, unassuming prayer, worshiping with or serving his congregation, and with children, a part of the human family of Quebec. While Cather acknowledges that his "large, drooping nose" and "grim, bitter mouth . . . might well have frightened a child who didn't know him," she goes on to distinguish hers from Parkman's Laval by depicting him as a man who would *not* frighten children who *do* know him. With the children in Notre Dame de la Victoire, for example, Cather's Laval is so approachable that Cécile asks him for coins for votive candles she and Jacques have lighted, and the prelate looks upon both of these children with stern compassion.

The overall effect is that, despite his many years as patriarch of his church, Cather's Laval is himself a preserver of an ancient domestic order as a most devoted minion of Mary. In this he is another important strand in the tapestry of domestic and spiritual tranquility Cather weaves around Cécile's life in particular and Quebec in general. At his appearance with Cécile and Jacques, just cited, Laval is praying in the Notre Dame de la Victoire Church, a church Cather describes through Cécile's eyes as "peculiarly the church of childhood." The spiritual father of his people, Laval is associated to Cécile with the Notre Dame de la Victoire Church, so named because of the contribution of another symbolic father of the colony, Count Frontenac, and his indebtedness to Mary's aid in defeating the British general Sir William Phips. Originally called the Church of the Infant Jesus, it is with this name that Cécile still associates the church and its connection to Laval. Cather writes:

> The furnishings and decorations which had been sent over from France were appropriate for a church of that name. . . . The high altar was especially interesting to children. . . . It was a representation of a feudal castle, all stone walls and towers. . . . Cécile had always taken it for granted that the Kingdom of Heaven looked exactly like this from the outside and was surrounded by just such walls. . . . She had taught Jacques to believe the same thing, and it was very comforting to them both to know just what Heaven looked like,—strong and unassailable, wherever it was set among the stars. (SOR, 63–65)

In her descriptions of the altar, Cather also associates Mary with this church, reinforcing her role as the mother of the colony and emphasizing her connection with Laval, father of the church in Canada as Mary is its mother. On the central of three stone towers in the church, Cather writes, rising "almost to the roof of the church, the Blessed Mother and Child stood high up among the shadows. . . . She was by far the loveliest of all the Virgins in Kebec, a charming figure of young motherhood. On her arms is a "little Jesus . . . so intelligent and gay, a child in a bright and joyful mood, both arms outstretched in a gesture of welcome, as if he were giving a fête for his little friends and were in the act of receiving them" (SOR, 65–66). By placing Laval above Jacques and Cécile in these passages, Cather draws a further comparison between this family and the Virgin and infant Jesus; she also makes plain that Laval, however potent a patriarch, is most willingly subject to Mary in his devotion to her and to her church. He is more than a simple minion or earthly representative of her love, however. Cather's Laval, by his careful ministration to the poor, discussed in greater detail in the next sections, in feeding, clothing, and washing those in need, is an agent of mercy, like Mary, and an exemplar of the loving care often traditionally associated with womanly nurturing. As part of a New World heroic that transcends discrete and limited orders, Laval's character enhances the family concept of Quebec that may be the truest reason *Shadows* was a comfort to Cather.

Even as unfriendly a chronicler of the progress of the church in New France as Francis Parkman also recorded the strong connection between the bishop and Notre Dame de la Victoire as an example of the prelate's fealty to Mary. To Parkman this is a bond that, ironically for the historian's conception of Catholicism, not only humanized Laval, by moving him beyond his typically dominant, patriarchal role, but which also elevated Mary by adding mundane power to her intercessional and maternal mercies. Parkman relates the bishop's and entire colony's humility before Mary, after Phips's defeat and at the time of the renaming of the church, in Laval's saying, "'We appealed to God, his Holy Mother, to all the Angels, and to all the saints.'" The historian goes on to add his own assessment of the grateful colony's position before Mary, writing:

Nor was the appeal in vain, for each day seemed to bring some new token of celestial favor; and it is not surprising that the head-winds which delayed the approach of the enemy, the cold and the storms which hastened his departure, and, above all, his singularly innocent cannonade, which killed but two or three persons, should have been accepted as proof of divine intervention. It was to the Holy Virgin that Quebec had been most lavish of its vows, and to her the victory was ascribed.[10]

Cather makes even more of Parkman's historic connection between Mary and the colony in her own fictional description of the familial recognition that passes between the old bishop and Jacques in Notre Dame de la Victoire. Cécile sees them "regarding each other in silence, but very intently," with Jacques, "his finger in his mouth, looking up at the Bishop shyly, but in a way that struck her as very personal" (SOR, 69). The bishop's internal monologue which follows, and the relation in which it places him to Jacques and the others in his congregation as truly the vicar of Christ, underscore both the filial belonging Cather created in her novel of French Canada and in her adaptation of historical accounts to achieve her ends; these passages also obscure conventional boundaries of nurturing solace commonly associated with female heroes, and so not only suggest but also transcend mere indebtedness by Cather to the power of the "Christian matriarchy" that, to Donovan, enriches Jewett's best New England fiction. Cather's transcendence of traditional distinctions is exemplified in the qualities she gives her fictional Laval. She imbues him with a generous love that encompasses a son's humility, a mother's tending of the young, and a father's sense of outraged justice. Such a richly layered rendering of his character helps Laval exemplify the order Cather presents as her standard for a new world and shows the blurring of class and gender she posited as essential to such a world.

For this building of character, Cather, not satisfied with Parkman's generally damning portrayals of Laval, or even with such occasionally neutral depictions as his humility to Mary just cited, turned to more sympathetic biographies of Canada's first bishop like Abbé Henri A. Scott's *Bishop Laval* for the 1926 Anniversary Edition of *The Makers of Canada* series and Adrien Leblond de Brumath's *Bishop Laval* in the 1910

edition of the same series.[11] Although both writers praise Laval's generosity to the poor, with de Brumath saying that "few
saints carried mortification and renunciation of terrestrial
good as far as he" and that "he used his whole substance in
alms and pious works,"[12] it is Scott who records the incident
on which Cather would base Laval's encounter with Jacques.
Scott writes:

> But while he was so cruel to himself he proved most kind to others.
> He had a small store of stuffs,—linen, blankets, clothes,—which
> he bought out of his little savings, and his greatest pleasure was
> to give them to the poor, who were always welcomed by him and
> who, with material help, always received a piece of pious and
> paternal advice. Once he met on the street in winter time a poor
> child half-naked and shivering with cold; he led him to the priest-
> house, washed and kissed his feet, gave him shoes, stockings, a
> complete suit of clothes and sent him home as content as himself.[13]

Cather transformed and expanded this material into an inset
story that conveys the tone of Laval's societal family of New
France and makes the prelate a personification of the larger
love of that order. She describes a cold night in January, when
Jacques, four years old and left unattended by his mother
'Toinette, awakes to a cold and empty house and goes, half-
clothed, into the streets to find her. He is found instead by "Old
Bishop Laval, who never spared himself" and who had been
out this night sitting with a sick woman, and is taken to the
humble rooms where the bishop "lived in naked poverty"
(SOR, 72–73). Cather closely parallels many historical details
in her narrative, from her fictional bishop's indigence, to his
selling of his own noble family's silver plate to feed and clothe
the poor, to his washing and kissing of Jacques's feet (SOR,
73–74); she personalizes her account, however, by telling her
story not in Abbé Scott's ostensibly objective third person, but
rather through Jacques's eyes, "in flashes, unrelated pictures,
like a dream" (SOR, 70). She also moves beyond Scott by iden-
tifying the half-clad boy, making him a fully sketched character with a family history, and, in so doing, creating a familial
connection between Jacques and the prelate which she completes through Laval's obvious love for the boy, a love based
on clothing, feeding, and warming.

This encompassing love is a defining aspect of the character of Cather's Laval, and one the significance of which cannot be overstated. The simple act of bathing another's feet, for example, has been described by Ann Romines as one of the "most eloquent acts" a compassionate human can perform.[14] The tending of feet that Romines specifically praises, occurs in "Old Mrs. Harris," as the nearly mute Mandy achieves perfect expression by offering the dying old woman "the greatest solace of the day . . . [the] something that Mandy gave, who had nothing else to give."[15] To Romines, this seemingly base act is tinged with "religious as well as domestic resonance" and "comes from the deepest levels of humanity."[16] Similarly, to Cather and the reader of *Shadows*, Laval is ennobled by his self-abasing kindness to the impoverished and neglected Jacques, further suggesting the dignity this prelate gains by his nongender and class-bound actions.

In drawing Laval's complex nature through scenes like these, Cather as effectively transcends what might be considered traditional maternal or spiritual love based on nurturing by supplementing it with the conventional attributes of fatherly justice. She writes of Laval's confrontation with the boy's mother:

Resolution
The Bishop came in without knocking, and motioned his man to put the child down and withdraw. He stood for some moments confronting the woman in silence. 'Toinette was no fool; she felt all his awfulness; the long line of noble blood and authority behind him, the power of the Church and the power of the man. She wished the earth would swallow her. . . . He meant to watch over this boy, he said; if she neglected him, he would take the child and put him with the Sisters of the Congregation, not here, but in Montreal, to place him as far as possible from a worthless mother. (SOR, 76–77)

The boy, in the care of Laval as patriarch, would thus be taken away from an unnatural mother and put into the hands of a more loving one, the church as exemplified by Mary and her vicars on earth, the Sisters of the Congregation. In this scene, one complementary to Laval's bathing and clothing of Jacques, Cather adds traditional paternal attributes to Laval's character; she also makes him more firmly the spiritual head of the

supportive larger family she envisioned through his filling the
role of the just parent, as he had earlier of the ministering lord
and nurturing mother.[17]

As Cather borrowed only slightly from Parkman and much
more heavily from Scott and de Brumath in adapting Laval
to fit these complex patterns of domestic unity, she also disre-
garded much from Laval's admirers that would weaken her
readers' perceptions of the prelate. She too mentions how he
relinquished his personal wealth such as the revenues from his
abbeys in France and transferred his vast Canadian land
grants to the seminary to live in poverty, how he allowed himself not even the creature comforts of fire in his room, and how
he rose each morning at four to enter the cold church and ring
the bell that would call Quebec to church (SOR, 73–74). But
she stops short of commending Laval's wearing of hair shirts
described by de Brumath, or his eating only of "a soup, which
he purposely spoiled by diluting it amply with hot water, a
little meat and a crust of very dry bread" and drinking "only
hot water slightly flavoured with wine."[18] In language that
ironically recalls Parkman's indictments of the prelate's exag-
gerated humility, de Brumath praises Laval's unstinting service to the poor, describing his work at the hospital where

> he even rendered them services the most repugnant to nature.
> ... When he thus attended the sick who were attacked by conta-
> gious fever, he did his duty, even more than his duty; but when he
> went, without absolute need, and shared in the repugnant cares
> which the most devoted servants of Christ in the hospitals under-
> take only after struggles and heroic victory over revolted nature
> he rose to sublimity.[19]

De Brumath explains this "indulging in the luxury of heroism
so repugnant" as a lesson to "those incurable and desperate
cases that they were the first friends of Jesus Christ, that the
Church looked upon them as its jewels, and that their fate from
the point of view of eternity was enviable to all."[20]

Cather praises Laval's austerity while omitting de Brumath's attention to the "repugnant cares" that must be overcome by a "revolted nature." As a result, her Laval is a
dignified prelate and worthy embodiment of the order that
informed the community of *Shadows*. Her selectivity in en-

hancing the giving but refined nature of her character also allowed Cather to reject many of the details of Laval's mortifications recorded by Scott; of his bed which was "a simple mattress on hard boards without sheets," from which "he did not suffer fleas to be shaken from his poor woolen blankets," for example, or of the meat he sometimes ate "that had been cooked eight days before and was at times swarming with worms." Scott's Laval, who "mortified all natural inclinations and deprived himself of all bodily comfort,"[21] is not the lordly prelate of *Shadows*, the man whose love transcends distinctions of class and gender, while his life and responsibilities are paradoxically shot through with such traditions. As such a symbolic character, Laval brings a communal stability to *Shadows*, the strength of the larger order of religion to create the family of Quebec in which individuals like the Auclairs and Jacques are as important to the social order as that order is to their private worlds.

It is through the kind of deft characterization she achieved in the creation of Laval that Cather most fully embodies the free, expansive society also envisioned by her early mentor, Sarah Orne Jewett. In Cather's Quebec as much as in Jewett's Green Island or even Dunnet Landing, gone is what Helen Fiddyment Levy calls the "cultural ideal of the dominant individual,"[22] to be replaced by a balanced community that gives due credit to women's domestic culture. What results is a sense of cooperation among all members of society that produces no less than the "New American Jerusalem" and the "egalitarian community . . . [that] achieve[s] the promise of a new order in a New World."[23] Merrill M. Skaggs sees Cather's inclusiveness as no less important, and, indeed, as the embodiment of an almost monolithically medieval "myth structure [that] unified the most diverse elements of a culture."[24] To Skaggs, this New World order is best described as "a unified Kebecois kind of feeling about life developed by a cohering community that honored such citizens as a loving and daughter-nurturing father"; and as "a secure place, a world in itself . . . shaped by mothers who pass along necessary knowledge before they die, and by fathers—natural, governmental, and clerical—who live to care for their own."[25]

In her depiction of another symbolic father, Laval's civil

counterpart Count Frontenac, Cather further and with equal skill embodied the same encompassing and boundary-free New World Order. In her Frontenac, she as effectively developed a representative of the secular order as she had of the religious one with Laval. Frontenac exemplifies the importance of the political society to the nuclear family by showing the sustaining force of the count's worldly, strong arm behind the struggling Auclairs and their dependents. Cather succeeds in her portrayal of Frontenac by making him, even more than the spiritual Laval, the synthesis—of class, gender, and public and private realms—needed to bring forth a new culture.

He, along with Laval, serves as a pivotal figure in the novel, in the creation of the larger concept of family needed for the fruition of the isolated settlement. Both leaders epitomize the largeness Cather's New World vision demanded and possess the traits associated with Western patriarchal figures by modern researchers such as Carol Gilligan. These characteristics include stressing individual achievement over connection and the concept of "distinctive activity as [it] defines the standard of self-assessment and success," as well as an emphasis on "an ethic of right."[26] But Cather adds personal depth to the depictions of both men, and thematic unity to her novel, by imbuing them with attributes more commonly considered typical of Western women, according to Gilligan's findings. Gilligan writes:

> While the [typically male] ethic of responsibility rests in an understanding that gives rise to compassion and care.... [and while another researcher] McClelland reports that ... men represent powerful activity as assertion and aggression, women in contrast portray acts of nurturance as acts of strength.[27]

Cather in part achieves this synthesis in Frontenac's character by adding her own imaginative softening to Francis Parkman's account of the "Father of the People, Preserver of the Country."[28] In Parkman's Frontenac, Cather found a public man who, although best known for his military glory, was also the subject of anecdotes that may have inspired Cather to portray him as a parent to the citizens of Quebec. Parkman writes:

> It was not in his instinct to clash with the humbler classes, and he generally reserved his anger for those who could retort it. By

fits he could be magnanimous. A woman once brought him a petition in burlesque verse. Frontenac wrote a jocose answer. The
woman, to ridicule him, contrived to have both petition and answer slipped among the papers of a suit pending before the council.
Frontenac had her fined a few francs, and then caused the money
to be given to her children.[29]

For Parkman, however, much more than for Cather, this protective, almost familial side of Frontenac is just one aspect of
the man both writers depict as one of the great anchors of
Quebec's security and strength. Parkman's Frontenac is above
all a formidable warrior and deliverer of his people. The historian relates how, for example, under severe threat from British
forces in October of 1690, "shouts, cheers, and the waving of
hats greeted the old man as he climbed the steep ascent of
Mountain Street. Fear and doubt seemed banished by his
presence."[30] He conveys this confidence still more strongly
in describing how Frontenac saves the community from even
greater threats, such as the combined forces of the English and
Iroquois. "From the moment when the Canadians found a chief
whom they could trust, and the firm old hand of Frontenac
grasped the reins of their destiny, a spirit of hardihood and
energy grew up in all this rugged population," he writes; "and
they faced their stern fortunes with a stubborn daring and
endurance that merit respect and admiration."[31] Parkman further clarifies his view of Frontenac's importance to the colony
by summing up the state of New France before the count's
second appointment as governor, when he was already a very
old man.

> The post was not a tempting one to a man in his seventieth year.
> Alone and unsupported,—for the King, with Europe rising against
> him, would give him no more troops,—he was to restore the pros-
> trate colony to hope and courage, and fight two enemies with a
> force that had proved no match for one of them alone. The auda-
> cious count trusted himself, and undertook the task.[32]

Cather's Frontenac is a similarly powerful leader and warrior, but her count is a great public man who is nonetheless
part of the general family of Quebec and the particular family
of Euclide and Cécile Auclair. "The accident of being born next
the Count de Frontenac's house in Paris had determined Eu-

clide Auclair's destiny," Cather writes, adding that the count found among those socially beneath him "the only human ties that were of any comfort to him" (SOR, 27). He is particularly close to the Auclair family in his Paris neighborhood, often dropping in "at the pharmacy to see his tenants, the Auclairs . . . [sometimes talking] to the old grandfather about his campaigns in Italy and the Low Countries" (SOR, 28). His tie with Euclide grows even stronger as, on his last stay before taking the "pharmicien" and his family to Canada with him, "he often sent for Euclide to come to him in a professional capacity,—a flimsy pretext, for, though past sixty, the Count was in robust health" (SOR, 31). Cécile, too, feels a great fondness for the old count, remembering him as "one of the important figures in her life," someone on whose knee she liked to sit when young and as the man who "beckoned Cécile with a long forefinger, put his arm about her familiarly, and drew her close to his side" (SOR, 57). He is the man to whom she appeals for money for shoes for Jacques, as she appeals to the old bishop for twenty sous for votive candles, fearing no rejection (SOR, 58), and the man who wills Cécile a dish of glass fruit which as a child she admires "more than anything I have ever seen" (SOR, 59).

Cather's is a warm portrait of a man whose feelings of protective affection make him a spiritual parent, with nurturing characteristics that defy traditional maternal or paternal distinctions; whose vitality extends to all of his people, especially to Euclide and Cécile and, through Cécile's love for the fatherless child, to Jacques. She achieved the complexity of character her fiction required by presenting Frontenac in the last months of his life, with his triumphs seen in memory and Cécile recalling how "five years ago . . . the Count had driven off Sir William Phips's besieging fleet" (SOR, 64). Even Euclide Auclair, although he sees the aging count as "more like a man revolving plans for a new struggle with fortune than one looking back upon a life of brilliant failures" (SOR, 239), must finally accept the prospect of Frontenac's death and assign him a place in "the old order . . . [whose] time has gone by" (SOR, 261). Auclair also remembers the count's youth, when Frontenac was a noble patron of the apothecary's own family who lived beyond his means, quarreled with his peers and superiors, and became a soldier at age fifteen, a career in which, though he excelled, "in each campaign he added to his renown, but never to his fortune" (SOR, 28).

Frontenac is of course no mere warrior of faded glory; he is at times for Auclair the last refuge of strength, the force that kept him from being "wholly and entirely cut off from France; a helpless exile in a strange land" (SOR, 263), as he is for Cécile "that feeling of security . . . the strong roof . . . over her and the shop and the salon and all her mother's things" (SOR, 265). Frontenac, for Cather, is primarily "the audacious count" that Parkman so admired. But he is also much more than this. Cather honored him for his role in creating, with Laval, a new society in which nuclear families such as the Auclairs and the Pommiers could exist apart from and yet connected to those around them, and in which the private domestic world of an apothecary's shop could add as much to the social and cultural fiber of a settlement as could the sway of potentates as large as Bishop François de Montmorency de Laval and the Count de Frontenac.

Such a balanced, connected world was of course not without its dangers and opponents. As Parkman writes, "Canada was entering a state of transition. . . . The epoch of the martyrs and apostles was passing away, and the man of the sword and the man of the gown—the soldier and the legist—were threatening to supplant the paternal sway of priests."[33] In *Shadows*, Cather successfully frames the present world of Cécile and the domestic center she creates around her by both the passing age of "martyrs" like Jeanne Le Ber and Mère Catherine de Saint-Augustin, and by the impending discord of a new breed of priests like Laval's successor Jean Baptiste de Saint-Vallier. Although to historians like Francis Parkman Saint-Vallier symbolized the same power-mongering as Laval, to Cather he represented the folly of personal pride that would most threaten the domestic tranquility of Quebec, as of all of Cather's later, endangered frontiers. Her Monseigneur de Saint-Vallier is the antithesis of her Laval, "a man still young," as opposed to Laval's nearly monumental age, "of a handsome but unstable countenance," in contrast to Laval's ancestral dignity, "clad in a black cassock with violet piping, and a rich fur mantle," in even greater contrast to the old bishop's thin and worn garb (SOR, 117).

His personality and ambitions for himself and his church in Canada are similarly at odds with those of Laval. "'Change is not always progress, Monseigneur'" (SOR, 119), Auclair tells the new bishop, reflecting on a course of action which "reverse[d] entirely Laval's system for the training and government of the Canadian clergy, thus defeating the dearest wishes of the old man's heart and undoing the devoted labour of twenty years" (SOR, 120). The changes Cather cites are most pernicious to her because they weakened the central position of Laval's seminary in favor of a movable clergy. "The Seminary, which Laval had made a thing of power and the centre of ecclesiastical authority, a chapter, almost an independent order, was now reduced to the state of a small school for training young men for the priesthood" (SOR, 120), Cather concludes.

This note of discord in the communal web Cather has created around Laval symbolizes the dilemma in a book often criticized as plotless or lifeless. For Cather and her readers, the drama lies in the young prelate's egoistical assertion. He is the individual, choosing to break with the community Laval has built, just as earlier in the novel he has chosen to abandon the old bishop's humble clerical residence for a private place. Cather's descriptions of Saint-Vallier's actions amount to such a lament as a family threatened with the loss of its traditional center might make. Her familiarity with the *Jesuit Relations* further helped her convey Laval's bitter disappointment over Saint-Vallier's actions. Her fictional accounts echo passages like these from the *Relations*, written by an embattled clerical opponent of the new bishop. "His predecessor, monsieur de Laval, who sees all this, is a holy man, and says that he was greatly deceived when he divested himself of his bishopric in favor of him who, contrary to his expectations, harasses us . . . and seeks only to humiliate the religious."[34] Later in the volume, the same cleric goes on to accuse Saint-Vallier, for his autocratic tendencies to all religious who opposed him, of causing an "ecclesiastical war . . . [that] is worse than the Iroquois war, on account of the scandal, and of the difference between the present times and those that existed . . . among the ecclesiastics and the religious [who were formerly of] cor unum et anima una."[35]

In history as in Cather's fiction, Saint-Vallier posed a threat not only to Laval's established religious order but to Frontenac's civil authority as well. With Frontenac, Saint-Vallier quarreled fiercely over the brandy trade and the moral tenor of the entire colony under the count's leadership. Cather presents this struggle most succinctly, by showing two encounters between Saint-Vallier and Euclide Auclair, one of the recipients of "the overtures [Saint-Vallier] occasionally made to people who were known partisans" (SOR, 120) of Laval and Frontenac.

Historically a manipulative and dramatic man, Saint-Vallier was accused, even by other religious like the correspondent in the *Jesuit Relations* just quoted, of treating "me like a little school-boy; he put many questions to me. . . . He acted like a man of the court, treating me to a rigmarole in order to entangle me, and, in the event of his being unsuccessful, to cast blame on me."[36] With Auclair, Saint-Vallier attempts the same practices, in an early meeting at which he questions the apothecary's treatment of Laval and, in an even more revealing scene, when he later questions and attempts to intimidate Auclair about the state of the dying count's soul, in this instance in regard to Frontenac's countenancing of the selling of brandy to the Indians as a necessary evil of the fur trade. "If the Count's illness is as serious as it seems to me, Monsieur Auclair, he should be given an opportunity to acknowledge his mistakes before the world as well as to Heaven," Saint-Vallier threatens Auclair. "Such an admission might have a salutary influence upon the administration which will follow his. Since he relies upon you, it is your duty to apprise him of the gravity of his condition." Auclair, whose sympathies clearly rest with the agents of an old order, "met Saint-Vallier's glittering, superficial glance and plausible tone rather bluntly" (SOR, 257).

Saint-Vallier's shallow aspirations meet an even more unyielding foe, time itself, as, at the end a thirteen-year period of exile and captivity, he returns in the epilogue as a broken and humbled man. He is no longer "a very young man of forty-seven . . . [but] a very old man of sixty." Cather depicts him as reduced by his shattered pride even more than by age, a "heavy, stooped, lame old man . . . [who] carried his head like a man broken to the yoke" (SOR, 270). Yet in his acceptance of his "leaden mantle of humility" (SOR, 272) Saint-Vallier achieves a nobility for Cather, coming even to resemble the predecessor he now humbly acknowledges in his own heart's fondest wish to abandon his episcopal palace in favor of a small apartment in the Hôpital General with its duties as hospital chaplain. These duties, the bishop tells Auclair, are

> very congenial to me . . . to celebrate the morning mass for the sisters and to hear their confessions; to administer the consolations of the Church to the sick and dying. As chaplain I shall be in daily attendance upon the unfortunate, as is my wish. (SOR, 274)

Not only has Saint-Vallier achieved the refinement of humility in Cather's depiction, but he has also learned an even more important lesson from his master. No longer working alone and to undo the work of those who came before him, Saint-Vallier returns chastened and one with his people. His reward is freedom from the emulation of the grandeurs of France, and the birthright as a citizen of a new order to share with Auclair the joys of watching Cécile's four sons, "the Canadians of the future,—the true Canadians" (SOR, 278), grow. He, too, as had Laval before him, comes to feel at one with the French Canadian culture about him, from his pain-heightened vision congratulating Auclair on having the wisdom to remain "here where nothing changes. Here with you I find everything the same," safe from the terrors in Europe where "the old age is dying, but the new is still hidden" (SOR, 277).

Saint-Vallier thus comes to share a place in a new familial, domestic, and social order, one equally informed by the careful ministrations of Cather's ultimate domestic artist and by the noblest pioneers Cather was to place on New World soil. In this apotheosis, Saint-Vallier joins Cather's other great historical figures who do not simply fall back into the void they have given their lives to fill, but who instead become part of a new culture of hope. In writing with an optimism which belied her anguish during a time of personal trial, Cather created for her readers the frontier produced by the union of Cécile and Pierre Charron. It is a world in which authority no longer comes simply from the "parchment and seal" of a past king, but "from knowledge of the country and its people . . . and from a kind of passion" (SOR, 268). In this home of the "Canadians of the future," more than in any other place Cather knew, she could build around Cécile "the quite centre" that she herself so longed for and admired.

4

The Central Role of Cécile and Her Domestic Art in *Shadows on the Rock*

To fully understand the cultural permanence Cécile represents in *Shadows on the Rock* the tradition in which Cather was working in the novel must be considered. From Jewett, she acquired love and respect for the culture and fine traditions that gave northern New England and neighboring Quebec their unique character. Her fiction, like Jewett's, also portrays the power of a communal matriarchy, with critics like Susan J. Rosowski and Hermione Lee seeing this social system so fully developed in *Shadows* as to make Cécile a Canadian Holy Mother.[1] Such interpretations help explain Cécile's artistry of the home and the Marianism Cather employs in the novel, although her larger conception of domesticity as a quality transcending the private world also merits exploration. Consideration of Cather's fiction in light of her concept of the extended social family of *Shadows* makes the distinction she draws between Cécile and Jeanne Le Ber even stronger, especially when set against the larger literary context of characters like Jewett's "Poor Joanna."[2]

Cécile's contribution to the domestic and family structure of Quebec as a legacy from the late Mme Auclair is an important aspect of *Shadows* as well as of Cécile's particular character. What Mme Auclair leaves Cécile, Cather writes, is "something so precious, so intangible; a feeling about life that had come down to her through so many centuries and that she had brought with her across the wastes of obliterating, brutal ocean. The sense of 'our way,'—that was what she longed to leave with her daughter."[3] "'Our way,'" in the larger context of the novel, is not simply the character of one family, but of the best of the entire colony. In the same passage, Cather makes the legacy even more important as she points out that the tradition Mme Auclair is passing on is a matriarchal inheritance. "The individuality, the character, of M. Auclair's house . . . was really made of very fine moral qualities in two women; the mother's unswerving fidelity to certain traditions, and the daughter's loyalty to her mother's wish" (SOR, 25–26).

These lines suggest that what Cécile accomplishes through her painstaking care is no less than the building of what Helen Fiddyment Levy has called "a revolutionary, more truly democratic American order" and "the New American Jerusalem."[4] This revolution is accomplished by the centrality of domesticity with its emphasis on "nurture" over "calculation" and "partnership" over "conquest."[5] In their role as domestic artists, women become key to "a distinctly American civilization" and providers of "a model to the society of more equitable human relationships and more vigorous cooperative social actions."[6] Merrill M. Skaggs sees Cécile's growing recognition of the sacredness of a well-tended daily life as representative of "a unified Kebecois kind of feeling about life"[7] and "a sacrament in which each element is an important and integral contributor to the whole," including the skillful performance of "humble chores."[8] And to Ann Romines, mastery of her art by a housekeeper like Cécile continues a ritual that fends off decay and lets the artist participate "in an enterprise connected with the continuity of a common culture and the triumph of human values over natural process. A housekeeper . . . beats back chaos every day with her broom."[9]

Such a sense of mission and inheritance grows in Cécile and shows the increasingly important contributions of a domesticity traditionally female to all inhabitants of Quebec. As Cécile matures more than the brief period of the novel's telling might seem to allow, she also comes to understand the legacy her mother bequeathed her. What might at first appear to be a child's retreat to a socially restricted female realm, for example, when Cécile lies ill in bed and considers the world around her, is in truth her acceptance of the importance of nurturance to a frontier colony. Cather writes:

> It was a pleasant and a novel experience to lie warm in bed while her father was getting dinner in the kitchen, and to feel no responsibility at all . . . her mind roamed about the town and was dreamily conscious of its activities and of the lives of her friends; of the dripping grey roofs and spires, the lighted windows along the crooked streets, the great grey river choked with ice and frozen snow, the never-ending, merciless forest beyond. All these things seemed to her like layers and layers of shelter, with this one flickering, shadowy room at the core. (SOR, 157–158)

Passages such as these, important in themselves, gain added strength as foreshadowings of Cécile's true epiphanies in the novel, first upon her return from the disturbing visit to the Harnois family on Ile d'Orleans, and finally when she openly acknowledges that not only is this house, the only home Cécile remembers, her home but that, on a far greater level, the savage rock of Quebec must forever remain her world. It is a world to which each individual, from such leaders as Laval and Frontenac to Cécile, mother of "the Canadians of the future" (SOR, 278), makes these contributions.

In her visit to the Harnois, Cécile, tired of the dirty clothes and bed linen and the family's coarse food, begs Pierre to take her back to the apothecary's shop where she can reflect, "they had kind ways, those poor Harnois, but that was not enough; one had to have kind things about one, too" (SOR, 197). These "kind things," Cécile learns from this visit, include everything from her clean apron to the carefully stocked supplies in her cellar and kitchen. It is also at this point that the previously nurtured child Cécile starts to become a consciously nurturing artist and adult. Cécile reflects,

> As she began handling her own things again, it all seemed a little different. . . . She did not feel like a little girl, doing what she had been taught to do. She was accustomed to think that she did all these things so carefully to please her father, and to carry out her mother's wishes. Now she realized that she did them for herself, quite as much. . . . These coppers, big and little, these brooms and clouts and brushes, were tools; and with them one made, not shoes or cabinet-work, but life itself. (SOR, 197–198)

From this realization of the importance of her routine actions, it is but a short step to Cécile's final insight about her life and where she chooses to live it, not back in France under the tutelage of her aunt but in the Quebec that has become her home. As the last ships leave for another year and Cécile and Euclide realize that they may never return to France, Cécile sits "not feeling dull, but happy and contented," using her "tools" to restore their home to the full luster it had enjoyed before it was threatened by the desertion of the voyage to France: under her renewed care, as Cécile polishes candlesticks and pewter cups and darns her father's counterpane,

> a little more colour had come back into the carpet and the curtains, she thought . . . she really believed that everything in the house, the furniture, the china shepherd boy, the casseroles in the kitchen . . . knew that . . . the world was not going to be destroyed this winter.

Cécile concludes that "a life without security, without plans, without preparation for the future, had been terrible" (SOR, 251–252). She also has learned how external forces—such as Count Frontenac's planned return to France—affect individuals, and how such private actions as polishing and darning can add luster to the societal fabric of the entire colony.

Cécile's convictions inspire her more timid father as well, so that Euclide comes to share his daughter's insights, and the small family's roots become firmly affixed to the New World soil. The relationship creates what Skaggs has described as "a secure place, a world in itself" which is "shaped by mothers who pass along necessary knowledge before they die, and by fathers—natural, governmental, and clerical—who live to care for their own."[10] It is also Cather's way of further exemplifying her New World order, in part, to Fiddyment Levy, by employing "a persistent plot circumstance in which European father . . . cedes the responsibility for the renewal of the family to his American-born daughter."[11] What results, as well as renewal, is an acceptance of the new home place that has previously been beyond the father's grasp. "'At home the old age is dying, but the new is still hidden,'" a chastened Bishop Saint-Vallier tells Auclair in the epilogue to *Shadows*. "'You have done well to remain here where nothing changes'" (SOR, 277). Also bolstered by the wisdom of his daughter and her husband, "the free Frenchman of the great forests" Pierre Charron (SOR, 171), Euclide acknowledges "that he was indeed fortunate to spend his old age here where nothing changed; to watch his grandsons grow up in a country where the death of the King, the probable evils of a long regency, would never touch them" (SOR, 280).

This closing reflection of the novel calls to mind the tone of acceptance that often marks Jewett's conclusions, especially that of *The Country of the Pointed Firs*. Because of her characters' adherence to traditions, ones often bequeathed to strong female heroes by their predecessors, Jewett's Maine, like Cather's Quebec, emerges as a region immune to the passage of time. Jewett's rural retreat becomes what Josephine Donovan calls "a place on the edge of historical time . . . an almost timeless female realm that stands as a counterreality to the encroaching male world of modern technology."[12] In part, *Shadows* also exemplifies such "a female realm," while it becomes something greater and more vital. Enduring as it is, the ideal "female realm" of Cather's Quebec exists not apart from or as an alternative to the central community, as the life of Jeanne Le Ber makes clear, but as an integral and interrelated part of a larger whole, and life in the northeastern frontier becomes more than an idyllic retreat. Cather's turning from Le Ber, from Mother Catherine, and finally even from Laval and Frontenac, to the complete and fruitful family of Cécile and Pierre for the novel's hopeful closing image, clarifies the larger order she conceived and the way she fashioned her own artistic vision from the lessons learned from Jewett.

A further connection between the worlds of Jewett and Cather can be observed by considering the strong Marian tradition Cather uses to build the rock of security that is Quebec and the heart of its culture. To the historians Francis Parkman and Abbé Scott and to the novelist Willa Cather alike, New France was a country uniquely dedicated to the Holy Family in general and to Mary in particular. For Cather, the matriarchal influence of the Holy Virgin is felt in two ways, first in the acknowledgment of Mary's authority by even her strongest male heroes, and secondly by the inset stories of intervention and salvation attributed to Mary in *Shadows*.

In the case of Bishop Laval, patriarch of the church in New France, reverence for Mary has already been illustrated in the prelate's piety in the Church of Notre Dame de la Victoire.

Several of the following inset stories also attest to Laval's Marian devotion. And, on the part of the proud civil authority Count Frontenac, the same allegiance to Mary is shown in the governor-general's deference as the glory for his victory over the British general Phips is given to Mary, prompting the renaming of a church in her honor. Through Cécile's thoughts, Cather makes it clear that such honor is freely given Mary by the people of Quebec.

> At Notre Dame de la Victoire one remembered the miraculous preservation for which it had been named, when this little church, with the banner of the Virgin floating from its steeple, had stood untouched through Sir William Phips's bombardment, though every heretic gun was aimed at it. (SOR, 95)

Similarly, despite his great courage and martial demeanor, Frontenac also accepts the role of the Church that has so venerated the Virgin Mother and built itself around principles of her divine intercession for both the living and the dead. "He would die here, in this room, and his spirit would go before God to be judged," Cather writes of the dying count. She adds,

> He believed this, because he had been taught it in childhood, and because he knew there was something in himself and in other men that this world did not explain. . . . In spiritual matters the Count had always accepted the authority of the Church; in governmental and military matters he stoutly refused to recognize it. (SOR, 247)

This admission not only shows Frontenac's devotion to Mary and her church, but also underscores the dilemma of his life and the promise of its solution in the New World Cather presents. He is essential to Cather's new standard in his embodiment of the old order of separation and male judgment, but as it is ameliorated first by his nurturing of those beneath him, and second, by his religious submission and connection to a spiritual community as he approaches death. Frontenac, again like Laval, points the way to Cather's new heroic, an order that Cather realizes by suggestion in the epilogue, in the union of the true Canadians, Pierre and Cécile.

Charron, in fact, comes to supplant even Frontenac as a symbol of strength and power. He is also a greater model of the domesticity and family structure that unite the community.

For Pierre Charron, Cather reveals through Cécile's perceptions, "It was clear enough that . . . the family was the first and
final thing in the human lot; and it was so engrafted with
religion that he could only say: 'Very well; religion for the
fireside, freedom for the woods'" (SOR, 174–75). In the distinctions they draw, both Charron and Frontenac express their
allegiance to the church, particularly to its matriarchal power
felt so strongly throughout New France and summed up by
Charron's "religion for the fireside" statement; and they dis-
play a degree of independence in keeping with Cather's "imaginative realism."[13] This independence places both men among
the ranks of Cather's respected, cultivated pioneers,[14] while it
is tinged with filial sentiments that enhance the strong familial
themes of *Shadows*.

Images of the family in *Shadows*, including the religio-
matriarchal themes discussed by Rosowski, Skaggs, Donovan,
and Lee, seem even more plausible in light of Cather's own
inset stories about Mary's power in the lives of the people of
Quebec. The intercession of Mary in saving the old sinner Marie, who perished in France but who was brought to redemption through the prayers of Mother Catherine in Quebec, has
already been discussed. A further direct appeal to Mary is cited
by Bishop Laval when he completes the image of the church
as a family by addressing a troubled Cécile as "'little daughter'" (SOR, 230) and tells her not to fear for Jacques if she
should be forced to leave Quebec. "'You must pray for him, my
child,'" Laval says. "'It is to such as he that our Blessed Mother
comes nearest. You must unceasingly recommend him to her,
and I will not forget to do so'" (SOR, 231). Answering her further objections, Laval adds, "'Our Blessed Mother can do more
for him than you or I. Never omit to present him to her compassion, my daughter,'" until "Cécile went away comforted"
(SOR, 232–33).

Cather enriches *Shadows* with many other stories about
Mary and the Holy Family, always with the goal of enhancing
the lives of the citizens of New France by making them part
of a larger order that makes their own fractured or incomplete
lives whole. Mme Pommier, for example, the crippled mother
of the cobbler who is making shoes for Jacques at Count Frontenac's expense, has a private chapel in her home on Holy

Family Hill that is dedicated to the Holy Family. As she tells Jacques,

> I am especially devoted to the Holy Family.... I insisted upon living here because the hill bore that name. My husband was for settling in the Basse Ville, thinking it would be better for his trade. But we have not starved here; those for whom the street was named have looked out for us, maybe. When we first came to this country, I was especially struck by the veneration in which the Holy Family was held in Kebec. ... I never knew its like at home. Monseigneur Laval himself has told me that there is no other place in the world where the people are so devoted to the Holy Family as here in our own Canada. It is something very special to us. (SOR, 101)

Even Blinker, the most deformed character in this novel that has been called "the author's personal purgatory,"[15] is restored through the symbolic power of the family, in this case the most sacred of Christian families. Cather describes the Auclairs' crèche and the curative power it holds for Blinker, or Jules, as well as for Jacques and the other townspeople who come to see it. "'Regardez, ma'm'sell,'" Blinker repeats over each newly unwrapped animal, until Cécile thinks that she "had never seen him come so far out of his shell; she had supposed that his shrinking sullenness was a part of him, like his crooked eyes or his red hair. ... the fête which she meant so especially for Jacques, turned out to be even more for Blinker" (SOR, 107). Blinker loses painful individuality even more completely as he becomes, while listening to Cécile's story of the Nativity, "another listener, by the fireplace behind her ... entirely forgotten ... until, with a sniffling sound, [he] suddenly got up and went out through the kitchen, wiping his nose on his sleeve" (SOR, 109). In this scene the central image is the Holy Family, with a Blessed Virgin who "wore no halo, but a white scarf over her head" and "looked like a country girl, very naive, seated on a stool, with her knees well apart under her full skirt, and very large feet" (SOR, 108).

In such simple images, reminiscent of the wooden statue of Mary that is, for Archbishop Latour's humble parishioners, "their doll and their queen,"[16] Cécile's crèche, with the familial power it represents, becomes the central metaphor of the novel. Blinker's road to temporal happiness begins most clearly in these scenes, as does Cécile's conscious nurturing of this unfortunate who becomes, along with Jacques and her father, one of Cécile's domestic dependents. Hermione Lee underscores the importance of these passages by describing the Nativity scene as "central to the book" with "Family life—of the right kind—re-enact[ing] the life of the Holy Family" and becoming for Cécile emblematic of the fact that "the literal, everyday life of the family has to maintain a metaphorical sanctity."[17]

In two related later narratives, Cather relies upon Blinker even more strongly as a measure of the restorative power and sanctity of the Holy Family manifested in the New World. Blinker's tears before the crèche, as he tastes his first freedom from the prison of self while regarding the Holy Family, also foreshadow his development in the later episodes. "'Don't you like to know that the angels are just as near to us here as they are in France?'"Cécile asks Blinker as he brings her news of a miraculous apparition to Jeanne Le Ber. "'Ma'm'sell, I think they are nearer'" (SOR, 129), he replies. Cather builds upon this growing, familial trust between Blinker and the Auclairs to complete her image of New France as the earthly ideal of mercy and justice, with the ameliorating Auclairs serving as a surrogate for the original Holy Family as well as citizens of the large community that embodies Cather's new heroic. On All Souls' Eve, Euclide has just told Cécile of the baseless torture and execution in France of the old knife-grinder Bichet, and of his own mother being so broken by the barbarity that "she had no wish to live longer in a world where such cruelties could happen." Moved by compassion and pride for the country she considers her true homeland, and unconsciously expressing the New World standard in which the political and domestic orders cannot exist apart, Cécile says defiantly, "'And I am like my grandmother. . . . I do not want to live there. I had rather stay in Quebec always! Nobody is tortured here, except by the Indians, in the woods, and they know no better'" (SOR, 93).

Cather builds upon this scene later in the novel, both to develop Blinker's character and to advance her portrayal of Quebec as a sanctuary in which daily life is grounded in eternal verities and unending life is promised even the humblest in the human family. After having overheard Auclair's earlier sympathetic account of Bichet's death, Blinker finds salvation and belonging in Canada along with the courage to lay bare his soul to the apothecary. He tells Auclair,

> I have wanted to tell you, monsieur, ever since All Souls' Eve. I came back late with my buckets, and the door there was a little open,—you were telling Ma'm'selle about the old man who stole the brass pots. I wanted to make away with myself—but you said something. You said the law was wrong, not us poor creatures. (SOR, 162).

In Auclair's response to the confession of Blinker, the king's unwilling torturer in the prison of Rouen, Cather completes her image of Canada as a place of salvation and hope, of a new world governed less by the abuses of human power than by the salvific forces of divine intervention and human connection. Her new standard of Quebec is also defined in this scene as a community in which lonely individuals and isolated or incomplete families are fulfilled by the conjunction of the private and public orders. As Cather makes clear, it is in Quebec that Blinker finds solace, through a restored faith in the humanity of a second holy family, that of the apothecary who had taken him in.

Both Blinker and Auclair, who throughout the novel longs for his return to France and feels cut off from the society he cherishes, gradually become less and less among "the unfortunate of this world." Rather, through an acceptance of a new order and their place in it, they move toward a belonging which characters like Cécile, Pierre Charron, and even Mother Catherine de Saint-Augustin have known during their entire lives in New France. Cather's carefully drawn sense of a community beneficently governed by an encompassing sacred and secular, political, and domestic order, then becomes the unifying vision of *Shadows*.

Narratives in *Shadows* that might at first appear unrelated also gain coherence through this interpretation, accounts like Pierre Charron's bitter lament about the wasted life of Jeanne Le Ber. With his piety toward the family, Charron is the oracle for Cather's harshest criticism in *Shadows*, words leveled against the noncommunal figure. Le Ber, like Jewett's "poor

Joanna," has become a recluse for religious purposes, as effectively taking herself out of her community as has Joanna on her island home. For her pains, Le Ber, like Joanna, also suffers a "spiritual aridity" that places her by the end of the novel, despite her former beauty and wealth, as more firmly among "the unfortunate of this world" than the outcast Blinker, who has moved within the healing circle of Cécile's domestic artistry and Laval and Frontenac's religious and civil protection. As importantly, the isolate Le Ber has also, unlike those who have learned to become part of the community around them, made her religion a bleak, unforgiving force, and not a familial tie with those around her.

In this, Le Ber is most at odds with Cécile, a character for whom religion and its miracles are sources of wonder and joy, as her union with Charron is the wellspring of new life and a new order as represented in her four sons, "the Canadians of the future" (SOR, 278). Cécile is truly the Canadian Holy Mother, both in her bringing forth of her corporeal offspring and, ultimately, of the new world they will create. And if Cather was inspired by Jewett's "community primarily . . . sustained by a kind of matriarchal Christianity and by other traditions of women's lore"[18] to conceive her own northeastern culture, she also wrote with her personal vision of the New World in mind—a vision in which family and domesticity were the exclusive provinces of neither men nor women, but where instead all classes and orders were part of a greater whole.

Such a sense of connectednes creates the atmosphere of Cather's novel, as it cements her ties to Jewett. The integration Cather achieved functions in part like the structure of Jewett's best work, *The Country of the Pointed Firs*, which gains much of its force from narrative that has been described as "webbed, net-worked," and "nuclear," or female-centered, rather than male-dominated or linear.[19] In considering these similarities and Cécile's thematic importance to *Shadows*, the findings of the theorist Carol Gilligan again underscore Cécile's role as the domestic center of the book. Cécile's symbolic nurturance of the entire colony can be viewed in Gilligan's terms of love, as originally summarized by the critic Elizabeth Ammons to describe Jewett's writing, as "an experience not grounded in separation [illustrated by the life of Jeanne Le Ber] and aggression [shown in one aspect of Laval's and Frontenac's personalities, and in their resulting conflicts] but in connections, in feelings of intimate relatedness to others."[20]

While it may be this relatedness that breathes life into *The Country of the Pointed Firs*, it is a similarly inclusive concept that makes the Auclairs' quaint home the center of Quebec for many of Cather's Canadian pioneers. That is, what is true of the worlds of Mrs. Todd and Mrs. Blackett is no less true of the domesticity of Cécile,[21] who shares her home first with her father and, to a degree, with Blinker and Jacques, and then with Pierre Charron and their four sons. Cather conveys this connectedness even more strongly in her epilogue. As well as Cécile and Pierre's vital family life, the incomplete nuclear family of Cécile's widowed father also continues to grow as Euclide shares his home with the adult Jacques, a sailor who stays in Cécile's former room when he is in port, almost as a son to Auclair.

The integration Cather achieved in *Shadows*, as well as Jewett's role in helping her attain such insights, has long intrigued scholars. Critics like Woodress, Donovan, Rosowski, O'Brien, Skaggs, Romines, Roman, and Fiddyment Levy, as just discussed, have made much of the aesthetic and cultural bonds between the two artists. Others have posited a seemingly paradoxical geographical kinship between Cather and Jewett, an affinity so central that it encompasses their shared sense of belonging in the Northeast. One researcher credits both the vastness of the authors' native environments and their responses to this size as principal reasons for the kinship. "In both Maine and Nebraska, Nature is overwhelming and vast, producing tight isolated little human communities which sprang up to foster survival," Beverly Gail Busch writes.[22] The question of survival is a real one, in the face of both Jewett's tractless ocean and Cather's equally fathomless prairie. For Jewett, the unsympathetic leagues can separate Joanna from even so small a community as Dunnet Landing, as they can deprive Mrs. Todd of her husband Nathan, who is lost "'just off shore . . . right in sight o' this headland.'"[23] For Cather, too, even in works which end by celebrating the region, the prairie can appear as a place in which "the world was left behind . . . over the edge of it, and . . . outside man's jurisdiction," and in which a character could feel "erased, blotted out" between "that earth and that sky."[24]

That both artists could see beyond such dark impressions and attain a knowledge leading to love of their regions attests to their common vision and belief in the need to learn of the world before writing of the parish. Such a connection is, at core, an understanding of the people of the regions—for Cather, of the diverse regions—that give the quality of life to fiction. Judged this way, Cather's mature writing, as much as that of the mentor she so praised in her introduction to *The Country of the Pointed Firs*, is marked with the "gift of sympathy" that makes the artist fade "away into the land and people of his heart, [so that she] dies of love only to be born again."[25]

5

Cather's Inheritance—and Sense of Peace—in Her Last Works

In her four major later works, two collections of long stories and two novels, Cather divided her artistic attention between the places she had considered home throughout her entire life. She returned in *Obscure Destinies* (1932), her first fiction after *Shadows*, to Nebraska for her characters and settings, as she did in her penultimate novel, *Lucy Gayheart* (1935). In *Sapphira and the Slave Girl* (1940) Cather reached further back, to her first home in Virginia. Yet even in this novel, which Cather described as so largely made up of old family and neighborhood stories that it was hardly fiction at all,[1] the ideals of New France and New England give the story a moral depth it could not have had had she merely relied on childhood memory. And in a still later work, the posthumously published *The Old Beauty and Others* (1948), although Cather set only one of the three stories in the Northeast, the region asserts itself both in a subtle shift of narrative point of view in "The Best Years," and in a direct use of setting and characterization in "Before Breakfast." "Before Breakfast" also gains significance by being her only fiction set on Grand Manan.

Central to these later works are family connectedness, though a connection not always as complete as that of *Shadows*, and the influence of Jewett. Cather seems particularly indebted to Jewett for much of the descriptive beauty of *Sapphira* as well as for a great deal of the characterization. Her world in the novel is in ways matriarchy, with power in the hands of two women, Sapphira Dodderidge Colbert and her daughter Rachel Blake. Another parallel between Cather's last novel and Jewett's fiction is found in the similarity between one of these characters, the benign medicine-giver Rachel Blake, and Jewett's herbalist Alvira Todd.

Before exploring Cather's treatment of her enduring themes in her last major work of fiction, *Sapphira*, a reading of *Obscure Destinies* and *Lucy Gayheart* is in order to understand the continuity of artistic subjects Cather carried with her from *Shadows*. The collective work *Obscure Destinies*—composed of the long stories "Neighbour Rosicky," "Old Mrs. Harris," and "Two Friends"—traces what might be called a descending arc of domestic comfort, from the almost beatific death of Anton Rosicky in "Neighbour Rosicky," as the dying man is nearly as reconciled to the earth as the earlier apotheosized Alexandra in *O Pioneers!* to Old Mrs. Harris, who also achieves a peaceful death, relishing the domestic order she has helped sustain, and her place in it; to the dissonant "Two Friends," in which two men allow their beautifully harmonized lives to sink into "a stupid, senseless, commonplace end."[2]

Anton Rosicky, a man who only in early middle age escaped an empty city life to become attached to the earth and to a sense of meaning, is described as someone with "one tap-root that goes down deep" (OD, 32). As a result, he and his wife Mary have produced a thriving farm and healthy, joyful children, as vital and naturally blessed as the children of Cather's first fully fleshed domestic artist, Ántonia Shimerda Cuzak. Their home is full of love and warmth and the good things a fruitful union can create: steaming breakfasts and rich coffee thick with cream; hot coffee cakes and apricot kolache; home-sewn clothing and feather pillows and quilts; and children nurtured on the fat of the milk, unlike their economical neighbors whose own offspring are, to a reproving Mary, "'pale, pinched little things . . . [that] look like skimmed milk'" (OD, 25). It is as if everything about the Rosickys' modest but orderly farm, including the nearly "homelike" cemetery (OD), exemplifies Cather's fictive ideal as explained by Ann Romines. "In 1931, with *Shadows on the Rock*, Willa Cather finally made a full entry into the life of housekeeping, as practiced by traditional women, and such housekeeping became a central concern of the last, great decade of her writing life."[3]

This literary dictum seems even more fully affirmed, though

with the foreshadowing of troubling resonances, in the collection's next story, "Old Mrs. Harris." Although perhaps none of Cather's other works, even *Shadows*, is more attuned to domestic rhythms and rituals than this one, discord is also inherent in the piece. At the core of the story is the conflict between Mrs. Rosen's housekeeping, marked by "superior cultivation which made everything she did an exercise of skill" (OD, 135), and the more joyous and "easy, cordial, and carefree" (OD, 111) ways of the Templetons. This benign rift can be seen in everything from the contrast painted in the story's opening lines between Mrs. Rosen's "own green lawn . . . [and] the ragged, sunburned back yard of her neighbours" (OD, 75); to the distinctions between the freely but often hastily served food at the Templetons and the "symmetrically plaited coffee-cake" (OD, 76) of Mrs. Rosen; and to the differing appearances of the Rosens' meticulous house and kitchen and even the "tightly corseted" (OD, 76) and perfectly groomed figure of Mrs. Rosen and their more overworked counterparts across the yard.

Still deeper discordances abound in the story, first between the Templetons and the neighbors who are less admiring of their charming ways than is Mrs. Rosen; and at a still deeper level, between members of the Templeton family itself. Cather's narrative seems to dismiss the galling neighborly jealousies somewhat more easily, as slights given at ice cream socials that underscore the distinctions between more ordered, "feudal" Southern ways and the expectations of a "snappy little Western democracy" (OD, 133) like Skyline, Colorado. By contrast, the generational tension between women of the same family seems more portentous, as even the reserved and dignified Mrs. Harris is at times reduced to lamenting that a discarded sweater from Mrs. Rosen "had become the dearest of . . . [her] few possessions" and was indeed "kinder to her . . . than any of her own children had been" (OD, 95). As bitter as this thought may be, Cather closes the story with a still more chilling, if prophetic one, about the fate of those linked most closely by blood. With the death of old Mrs. Harris, the simultaneously rejuvenating and battering currents of life will go on for those she leaves behind, Cather suggests, as she writes:

Thus Mrs. Harris slipped out of the Templetons' story; but Victoria and Vickie had still to go on, to follow the long road that leads through things unguessed at and unforeseeable. When they are old, they will come closer and closer to Grandma Harris. They will think a great deal about her, and remember things they never noticed; and their lot will be more or less like hers. They will regret that they heeded her so little; but they, too, will look into the eager, unseeing eyes of young people and feel themselves alone. They will say to themselves: "I was heartless, because I was young and strong and wanted things so much. But now I know." (OD, 190)

With the artistic precision a lifetime of writing had given her, Cather placed "Two Friends" immediately after "Old Mrs. Harris." And while "Old Mrs. Harris" ends on a somber note, the story is nonetheless an affirming one in many ways. In contrast, "Two Friends" seems completely colored by the loss and struggle that forms only one thread of the Templeton women's lives. Painful nostalgia underscores "Two Friends," from the opening line that hints at early disappointment—"Even in early youth, when the mind is so eager for the new and untried, while it is still a stranger to faltering and fear, we yet like to think that there are certain unalterable realities, somewhere at the bottom of things" (OD, 193)—to the closing line that is as remorseless as the ending of *My Mortal Enemy:*

When that old scar is occasionally touched by chance, it rouses the old uneasiness; the feeling of something broken that could so easily have been mended; of something delightful that was senselessly wasted, of a trust that was accidentally distorted—one of the truths we want to keep. (OD, 230)

In between, Cather unfolds the tale of a friendship squandered that is as rare as the occultation of Venus the story's principals witness together. And in the process, an "equilibrium" which is the young narrator's greatest security and joy, vanishes (OD, 227). Gone from the characters' lives, and from the world, the narrator implies, is "the silence,—the strong, rich, outflowing silence between two friends, that was as full and satisfying as the moonlight" (OD, 226). Dying with the friendship, for an ideological principle that becomes more important than human relations, is an anchor and order not to be found again. In the quiet telling of this tale, Cather completes her account of obscure destinies, as she moves further from the assurance she celebrated in *Death Comes for the Archbishop* and *Shadows* and metaphorically down the human path, perhaps, she describes best in "Old Mrs. Harris."

Her next long work, *Lucy Gayheart*, continued the dialogue to find meaning, both aided and hampered by the rich lessons life had taught a mature artist. In the novel's central character, Cather has created another motherless child, but one who is not informed by a rich maternal legacy as is Cécile Auclair. Also unlike another burgeoning artist, Thea Kronborg in *The Song of the Lark*, Lucy does not have the benefit of a sympathetic, living mother who will nurture her privacy and talent. What Lucy has instead is a life marked by failures of communication—between herself and a sister who despises both Lucy's grand aspirations and her smaller but as significant attachments, to an old apple orchard, for example, that symbolizes to Lucy "her beautiful memories . . . those feelings with which she had once lived"[4] in youthful hope and safety; between herself and Clement Sebastian, an aging and embittered singer who wants to forget, through Lucy's youth, that he is "without a country, without a home, without a family . . . and friends . . . [and, more importantly] the deepest of all companionships, a relation with the earth itself, with a countryside and a people" (LG, 78); and between Lucy and Harry Gordon, her oldest friend and the one who, perhaps, could do most to save her, both spiritually and, at the novel's climactic moment, physically. Lucy most needs to connect with Harry, if only "for old time's sake" and because he alone, in her town of Haverford, "knew the world . . . had some imagination . . . was alive" (LG, 174–75).

It is also to Harry that Lucy extends a final, desperate hand of not mere friendship but of an even more vital human connection. Such connection can never exist for Lucy in this world, however, Cather implies, and it is only in memory and reflection, symbolized by Lucy's fleeting footsteps encased in a cement sidewalk, that reconciliation is possible. And while some critics have implied that an artistry, the art of living, is at length achieved through memory in this novel, although by neither the vainly aspiring Lucy Gayheart nor Clement Sebastian, but by Harry Gordon,[5] the story is in most ways one of art failed and doomed by a lack of the interaction and belonging last seen in Cather's fiction in *Shadows* and, in part, in *Obscure Destinies.*

With *Sapphira,* Cather turned back to a vision and to a time colored by her earlier ordered and mystically unified vision as well as by the discord of a world marked by encroaching personal and, in the menacings of another world war, universal disarray. James Woodress describes part of the period of Cather's writing of *Sapphira* as "the hardest year in Cather's life," with the "devastating loss" of her brother Douglass in June of 1938 and Isabelle McClung Hambourg's death in October.[6] These were, Woodress writes, "the two people in the world dearest to her. Her brother . . . a twin, and Isabelle . . . the one for whom all her books had been written."[7] The start of World War II and the surrender of the French army also left her disconsolate,[8] and it was within this emotional climate that Cather finished writing *Sapphira.*

It is little wonder, then, that Cather returned to an earlier period of her own and the country's life, and why her depiction of human connectedness, even as it borrowed from Jewett's less ambiguous vision of domestic belonging, is problematic. As mentioned earlier, as Cather attempted to reconstruct a world she feared lost or at the least vanishing, she reached back to a descriptive power, a sense of characterization, and, in this creation of character, the healing touch of a medicine-giver, her own Rachel Blake, who is not unlike Jewett's Alvira Todd. Like Mrs. Todd, Rachel belongs to a family order larger than the nuclear one, as seen in her relation to Mrs. Ringer, a woman who was "born interested"[9] and who sends "a pale little girl, barefoot, in a carefully mended dress" (SSG, 117) to ask for Mrs. Blake's aid. Like most of Alvira Todd's clients, Mrs. Ringer requires less medical than personal attention, as Mrs. Blake acknowledges to herself. "Indeed . . . old Mrs. Ringer had sent for her because she had not seen her for a long time and wanted to visit with her" (SSG, 118). The visit to the Ringer's farm, like most of Mrs. Todd's journeys, is made on foot, through countryside distinctly Virginian though no less lush and fragrant than the rural Maine Alvira Todd and the narrator of *The Country of the Pointed Firs* travel through so appreciatively.

The attention to natural detail, common to all of Cather's work after she heeded Jewett's advice to "write it as it is,"[10] is as strong in this passage from her last novel as in any of her fiction:

> In the deep ravine below the road a mountain stream rushed coffee brown, throwing up crystal rainbows where it gurgled over rock ledges. On the steep hillside across the creek the tall forest trees were still bare. . . . From out the naked grey wood the dog-wood thrust its crooked forks starred with white blossoms—the flowers set in their own wild way along the rampant zigzag branches. . . . [Lost in thought as she viewed this scene, Mrs. Blake] gave scarcely a glance at the wild honeysuckle all about her, grow-ing low out of the gravelly soil, pink and rose colour, with long, trembling stamens which made each blossom look like a brilliant insect caught in flight. . . . From the Ridge road Mrs. Blake could look down over hills and valleys, as if she were at the top of the world. She liked to go up there at any time of the year, and she liked to go on foot and alone. Even in her best days, before her husband died . . . she used sometimes to be homesick for these mountains and the high places. (SSG, 115–17)

The nostalgic tone of such passages recalls Cather's early loneliness on the Nebraska prairie and the spiritual dichotomy in her life between the Western plains and the Eastern moun-tains. It also suggests the solution to her dilemma, an integra-tion, again, perhaps, learned from Jewett, of the artist and her materials that would culminate in the larger connection and order of *Death Comes for the Archbishop* and *Shadows*. That Cather learned to love her own country through her apprecia-tion of Jewett's treatment of the Northeast seems likely from Cather's praise of her mentor, in the preface she wrote to *The Country of the Pointed Firs*.

> If [the artist] achieves anything noble, anything enduring, it must be by giving himself absolutely to his material. And this gift of sympathy is his great gift. . . . He fades away into the land and people of his heart, he dies of love only to be born again.[11]

In both artists' treatments of the lands that mattered so much to them, natural things take on symbolic meanings and make the fiction resonate. For both Cather and Jewett, for ex-ample, pennyroyal and tansy work to restore or recall human ties that have been sundered. Often, in melancholy evocations of human bereavement in Cather's later works, those that follow *Shadows*, these plants recall thwarted loves or diminished lives. Mrs. Blake thinks of her dead husband as she sits atop a Virginia ridge in the passage just cited, and "Tansy Dave" is both a character and an inset story of grief carried to madness in *Sapphira*. In these instances, Cather, whether working instinctively from an artist's intuitions, purposely from memory, or unconsciously from metaphors learned from her mentor, employs the "scents of primeval herbs" to build upon ageless human suffering, the suffering of isolation and loss.

As just described, Mrs. Blake recalls her dead husband while she is walking through the blossoming hillsides of the Ridge. This scene is reminiscent of Mrs. Todd's musings to the narrator of *The Country of the Pointed Firs*, in the chapter, "Where Pennyroyal Grew."[12] "Among the grass grew such pennyroyal as the rest of the world could not provide," Jewett's narrator reflects, only to be told by Mrs. Todd,

> There, dear, I never showed nobody else but mother where to find this place; 't is kind of sainted to me. Nathan, my husband, an' I used to love this place when we was courtin', and . . . when he was lost, 't was just off shore tryin' to get in by the short channel out there between Squaw Islands, right in sight o' this headland where we'd set an' made our plans all summer long. (CPF, 48)

Powerful as this grief is, the pennyroyal recalls an even harder bereavement for Mrs. Todd. She confesses to the narrator:

> 'Twas but a dream with us. My heart was gone out o' my keepin' before I ever saw Nathan; but he loved me well, and he made me real happy, and he died before he ever knew what he'd had to know if we'd lived long together. . . . But this pennyr'yal always reminded me, as I'd sit and gather it and hear him talkin'—it always would remind me of—the other one. (CPF, 48)

Jewett's use of pennyroyal is especially symbolic in these passages in uniting a woman with both the beginnings of life, in her premarital courting, and with death. As Elizabeth Ammons points out, pennyroyal "is the special herb of women, specifically of womb," based on its use in childbirth, to help expel the placenta, and on its power "to induce or increase menstrual flow."[13] To Ammons, the symbolic use of pennyroyal in connection with the childless but nonetheless matriarchal Mrs. Todd makes the herb suggest "maternal power itself: the central awesome power of women, like the Earth, to give or not to give life."[14]

By employing a similarly mythical metaphor, Jewett heightens Mrs. Todd's grief by comparing her to "Antigone alone on the Theban plain. . . . An absolute, archaic grief possessed this countrywoman; she seemed like a renewal of some historic soul, with her sorrows and the remoteness of a daily life busied with rustic simplicities and the scents of primeval herbs" (CPF, 48). The archaic grief is human suffering and loss, the loss of an individual, in this case, or of a relationship with God and society, as Jewett treated it in her story of "Poor Joanna."

Cather's reference to tansy, in the "Tansy Dave" section of *Sapphira*, is a still more haunting tale of the pain human separation can cause, especially in a world no longer guided by the vision of a societal family order Cather posited in the Quebec of *Shadows*. "Tansy Dave" unites the sorrow of a man with the power of the "primeval herbs" in such a way as to move even Sapphira. Dave, a "half-witted ghost of a man" (SSG, 205) and a "scarecrow man, bare-legged, his pants torn away to the knee, his shirt a dirty rag" (SSG, 204), was once "one of the happiest boys on the place" (SSG, 205). His distress over losing a woman, herself a slave to a visiting woman from Baltimore, and his powerlessness in the face of slavery, maddens him. Tansy plays a doubly ironic role in Dave's life, serving first as a symbol of his hope as "he rolled over and over in the tansy bed, 'to make himself smell sweet'" before courting Susanna, and later as a mocking appellation of his feeble mindedness. Cather uses this inset story both to show the evil of slavery and to add ambiguity to the dark portrait of Sapphira, who finds herself "melted by the boy's desperation" (SSG, 206). The tale also recalls Jewett's pervasive use of herb imagery in her fiction and so helps forge the link between Cather as "'an American of the Apache period and territory'"[15] and her northeastern influences.

These influences are apparent in *Sapphira* in other, more direct ways, particularly in key allusions to Quebec as a world of hope for the oppressed in the South, a very escape "out of

Egypt to a better land" (SSG, 228). In this case, too, as in the epilogue to *Shadows*, the hope of a larger order or New World heroic is held out in French Canada by indirect telling and narration rather than by direct description or plotting. In a dark moment of recognition, Henry Colbert realizes that her Southern home is irretrievably lost to Nancy. "Every word his daughter said made him know Nancy could never be the same again," he acknowledges, "could never be happy here. He must face it" (SSG, 227). Colbert and Rachel Blake know that Montreal, despite its large population and exotic language, and in contrast to her familiar world of danger, holds for Nancy a human bond uncorrupted by slavery and as a result stronger even than the one she shares with her mother Till; a world of "many folks . . . that are a sight kinder than some folks on this farm" (SSG, 226). Having once admitted the truth of Sapphira's treachery, the miller sees the matter even more clearly, until he can only wish for Nancy to

> go up out of Egypt to a better land. Maybe she would be like the morning star, this child; the last star of night. . . . She was to go out from the dark lethargy of the cared-for and irresponsible; to make her own way in the world where nobody is altogether free, and the best that can happen to you is to walk your own way and be responsible to God only. (SSG, 228)

Such a fate, Cather's epilogue reveals, is exactly what awaits Nancy. These closing pages are also as succinct a statement of her new order as Cather gives in her fiction, including the chastened Saint-Vallier's praise for the steadfastness of Quebec at the end of *Shadows*. Nancy returns from Quebec twenty-five years later, a housekeeper to a wealthy colonel, perhaps, but "a tall, gold-skinned woman" in a fox-trimmed coat, wearing a black silk dress and gold watch (SSG, 283) all the same. She has a "charm about her voice," and a precise, elegant speech that her mother Till recognizes as "'just like [the cultivated English servant] Mrs. Matchem['s] down at Chestnut Hill!'" (SSG, 286). More important to the youthful narrator of the epilogue, "I liked the way she sat in her chair . . . and I liked to see her move about,—there was something so smooth and measured in her movements" (SSG, 284).

In her elegance in manner and dress, Nancy shows a cultural

influence Cather well may have remembered from her childhood but which also seems likely to have resulted from her
own mature knowledge of French Canadian tradition and the
value writers Cather admired, such as Sarah Orne Jewett,
placed on such refinement as a cultural trait of the Northeast.
This nobility also serves as a type of larger family resemblance
for Jewett, as the narrator of *The Country of the Pointed Firs*
indicates. She muses at the Bowden family reunion, at which
Mrs. Blackett, Mrs. Todd's mother, unofficially presides:

> I had been noticing with great interest the curiously French type
> of face which prevailed in this rustic company. I had said to myself
> before that Mrs. Blackett was plainly of French descent, in both
> her appearance and her charming gifts, but this is not surprising
> when one has learned how large a proportion of the early set-
> tlers on this northern coast of New England were of Huguenot
> blood.... "They used to say in old times that our family came
> of very high folks in France" [Mrs. Todd then tells the narrator].
> (CPF, 91–92)

Warming with a new respect for the Bowdens' "inheritance of
good taste and skill and a certain pleasing gift of formality,"
for "something that made them do all these things in a finer
way than most country people would have done them," the
narrator reflects, "their ancestors may have sat in the great
hall of some old French house in the Middle Ages, when battles
and sieges and processions and feasts were familiar things"
(CPF, 94–95).

In both Cather's and Jewett's fiction, this cultural and familial "inheritance of good taste and skill and a certain pleasing
gift of formality" manifests itself most clearly in the simplest
things, from Cécile polishing her father's brass candlesticks in
their home in Quebec, to Mrs. Blackett's sewing a shirt for her
son with "those dear old fingers and their loving stitches, that
heart which had made the most of everything that needed
love!" (CPF, 52), to Nancy wearing a fresh apron as she "in-
sisted upon helping Mrs. Blake and Moses' Sally in whatever
housework was under way" (SSG, 286). In such small gestures
Cather seems to have found the "quiet centre" of life as well
as the graceful traditions of a common culture. This center is
built upon early recollection, but also upon an inheritance of
ideas and places from mentors like Sarah Orne Jewett.[16]

This inheritance, to Ann Romines, further relates Nancy to Cather's earlier domestic artists through a shared language of housekeeping that "keeps Nancy connected with the home folks.'"[17] Romines further argues that Nancy's achievements and adhering to this most basic language let her exemplify not only the plot of liberation or discovery but also that of domestic ritual.[18] Even Cather's success in depicting such a domestic center at the end of *Sapphira*, however, does not destroy the memory of the wrenching disunity of Sapphira's pre-Civil War South. That is, although domesticity and New French inheritance indeed become Nancy's own, they do so only at the loss of her earliest home in the American South. Nancy, too, although she has become an artist of living and domestic skill, not unlike the earlier Cécile, both greatly resembles and differs from Cather's earlier artists. She is, until and perhaps despite her reconciliation with Till in the epilogue, in ways as motherless as Cécile; in fact, because of Till's early inability to protect her own child from Sapphira, and Nancy's forced learning of a new culture in French Canada, Nancy is in ways more deprived of a maternal heritage than Cécile.

Till, an orphan herself, also suffers domestic dislocation. To Romines, the English servant, Mrs. Matchem takes the place for Till that Mme Auclair does for Cécile, but with a difference that underlies the more ambivalent world of *Sapphira*. "Matchem's lesson is essentially that of Madame Auclair: that domestic order gives our lives beauty, security, and meaning, and is central to civilization," Romines writes. "And Till is a pupil at least as willing and apt as Cécile Auclair. But the civilization she preserves . . . conceives of Till as a piece of property; she is herself one of the household objects she puts in order."[19]

Yet by the end of *Sapphira*, it seems clear that the language of domesticity, however learned and transferred, is a universal one and one which plays its part in undoing the damage of a slave state's skewed values. In book 9, "Nancy's Return (Epilogue—Twenty-five years later)," Nancy and the post-Civil War freedom she represents, receive their own apotheosis at Cather's hands. It could even be argued that Nancy's triumph is more real if not greater than Cécile's, since we see her directly in the epilogue to *Sapphira*, as opposed to the indirect telling of Cécile's happiness in *Shadows*. As well as gaining dignity and refinement, Nancy has also maintained and in fact added to her previous domestic abilities.

Perhaps as significantly, Nancy can use the liberty her hard-earned refinement has won her to return to a free South and to reclaim her ties with her oldest friends and blood family, as is made clear by the shared viewing of "Till's keepsakes and treasures," including such things as Henry Colbert's books, Sapphira's lace caps and "odd bits of finery," and a brooch with a lock of hair from both Henry and Sapphira (SSG, 291–92). In the sharing of these objects and their stories of a common past, reconciliation is made both more moving and complex, and this last novel takes its place among Cather's more powerful, finished work.

Although Cather was to publish no new book-length fiction after *Sapphira*, the posthumous *Old Beauty and Others* offers additional insights into her vision of life and art as she faced her final decade. Increasingly assailed by illness, fatigue, and the horror of a world again at war, Cather nonetheless produced "Before Breakfast" in 1944 and "The Best Years" in 1945 ("The Old Beauty" was written in 1936 but unpublished until 1948). Surprisingly, despite the overriding darkness and sterility of the earlier title story, in both "The Best Years" and "Before Breakfast" Cather succeeded in reaching into her past to evoke a freshness of feeling and in further forging the ties with Canada and the American Northeast that helped sustain her through much of her later life.

Placed first in the volume and also serving as the title story of the collection, "The Old Beauty" is generally considered not representative of Cather's best style, as opposed to the other two stories in the volume. It is what James Woodress calls "definitely below Cather's usual mark" and void "of the old power of her best fiction to grapple the emotions."[20] Set in Aix-les-Bains after the First World War, the work is peopled with characters who seek the elegance, ease, and security of prewar Europe. Both Henry Seabury, the narrative voice of much of the story, and Mme de Coucy, formerly Lady Gabrielle Long-street, seem more at ease with the lost world of the past than with the present and with their fears for the future. Indeed, for Seabury, who is back in France after building a business career in China, Lady Longstreet symbolizes all that has gone out of the world. For him, her name itself recalls "a society whose manners, dress, conventions, loyalties, codes of honour, were different from anything existing in the world today."[21] It is precisely this nostalgia that Seabury seems to need most as, at the beginning of the story, he is "hunting for something, some spot that was still more or less as it used to be" (OB, 7). At Aix-les-Bains he finds such a place, "unchanged" and frequented by "many people very like those who used to come there" (OB, 7).

This reunion of Seabury and Gabrielle Longstreet is in ways rewarding, at least, to Cather herself, from a literary standpoint. Even after the story was viewed unkindly by Cather's longtime friend and the editor of *Woman's Home Companion,* Gertrude Lane,[22] Cather persisted, at least for a time, in her belief in the story's merit. There is also some human fulfillment in the tale, especially as Gabrielle recalls an act of Old World heroism, perpetrated years ago by a young Seabury who saved her from the forced advances of an unscrupulous banker. As if in writing a coda to her earlier *Lost Lady,* Cather provided in Seabury's actions a strength and poise of which Niel Herbert was incapable, when she records Gabrielle's praise of her youthful savior as "'so calm, with all a man's strength behind it [his decisive demeanor],—and you were only a boy'" (OB, 49).

Other more peaceful resonances occur within the book, both in Seabury's reflecting, of the now aged Lady Longstreet, that "it had struck him that she was living her life over again,— more understandingly than she lived it the first time" (OB, 37), and in the more balanced worldview of Gabrielle's companion, Mrs. Allison (Cherry Beamish). Of the main characters of the story, it is only Cherry who can be encouraged by contemporary people in a contemporary world. She alone can consider "'the present—which is really very interesting, if only you will let yourself think so.'" (OB, 31) as well as the past. But despite such images and counterpointing, "The Old Beauty" remains a backward-looking story, colored by Gabrielle's dashed hope that, "'once the war was over, the world would be just as it used to be'" (OB, 44).

During her own trials in the mid-1930s, just discussed, when she was writing both *Lucy Gayheart* and "The Old Beauty," and in the throes of a loss she seems to have confronted in both works, Cather may have felt such a world-grief as keenly as did Gabrielle Longstreet. An accident of publication after Cather's death, however, in pairing the earlier "Old Beauty" with "The Best Years" and "Before Breakfast," suggests how fully she had worked through her sense of life's dislocation in *Sapphira*. In her only completed works after *Sapphira*, she dealt with meaning and connection as completely as she had in many earlier works, and, as in them, by depicting the healing power of both memory and of a sense of domesticity that is tinged with the influence of Sarah Orne Jewett and the northeastern culture the two artists came to share. Indeed, Cather extended her connection with a northeastern culture by writing her only stories told through native New England narrative voices, "The Best Years" and "Before Breakfast." Both works are marked by a regional influence, in the choice of New England-bred Evangeline Knightly to relate the events of "The Best Years," a tale that Cather wrote, according to Woodress, "as a gift for Roscoe, a reminder of their life together when they were children in Red Cloud,"[23] and in her only use of Grand Manan as a fictional setting in "Before Breakfast."

In the complex "Best Years" Cather looked to her early Nebraska home for the story's domestic details, writing of a female protagonist who, like Cather's brother Roscoe, had taken a job teaching school to help her family financially;[24] and who, like Cather, according to Woodress, "is especially close to her oldest brother Hector, who is in action a practical, executive type but in mind something of a dreamer," a characterization which is "a pretty good likeness of Roscoe Cather."[25] Woodress points out other parallels such as the similarity between Cather's mother and early home and their counterparts she creates for Lesley Ferguesson. Mrs. Ferguesson, he says, has "a good bit" of Mrs. Cather in her, especially in her "strong, forceful personality," while the Ferguessons' home "is a replica of the story-and-a-half frame house the Cathers lived in on Cedar Street."[26]

Yet even as Cather reached back to reconstruct her early Nebraska memories in this story, she did not choose for her narrator a Western-reared Jim Burden or Nellie Birdseye or Niel Herbert, but instead the Brunswick, Maine, native Evangeline Knightly. Twice Cather refers directly to Miss Kightly's

New England heritage (OB, 78 and 127), and a third time, to emphasize the attractions of a Lincoln hotel to a Miss Knightly who superintends a rural school district, Cather writes, "She was New England born and bred, too conscientious to stay in the city for mere self-indulgence, but quite willing to be lost to MacAlpin and X—County by the intervention of fate" (OB, 119). It is not likely that such insights into the character of her narrator could be based entirely upon her childhood recollections of a favorite teacher; these traits seem to be instead the mature Cather's insights into a tradition she had come increasingly to accept as her own. This projection is especially significant if the vibrant protagonist Lesley Ferguesson is to be viewed, as Cather said of her best-known female hero, Ántonia Shimerda, as "'a rare object in the middle of a table, which one may examine from all sides . . . because she *is* the story,'"[27] and the narrator through which the author expresses her inmost wonder at her creation is no longer the Western Jim Burden but, in Cather's later years, the New Englander Evangeline Knightly. Cather completes her identification with the Northeast by describing Miss Kightly's return to "the scenes of her childhood" in Maine (OB, 127) rather than the Nebraska prairie on which earlier characters like Jim Burden find their own "precious . . . incommunicable past."[28]

As strong in this story as the New England influence is Cather's attention to home and hearth. The Ferguesson house itself is a "covenant" to the family, with mother and children being bound to it and to each other with "the deepest, the most solemn loyalty . . . [in] a consciousness they shared . . . [which] gave them a family complexion" (OB, 104). This "complexion" is particularly evident in many aspects of the family members and the spaces they have created for themselves: in the Upstairs, which is for the children "a story in itself, a secret romance" and "their very own world" (OB, 106–7); in the back porch floor, on which Lesley "sank into idleness and safety and perfect love" (OB, 112); in the bond between her brothers and Lesley which renders them "telepathically one" (OB, 94); and in Lesley's "feeling of being at home," which makes her like a "plant that has been washed out by a rain storm . . . when a kind gardener puts it gently back into its own earth with its own group" (OB, 96–97). In these descriptions of the home place, as much as in the narrative passages just quoted, Cather's literary heritage and her own unique legacy seem to be as consummately expressed as in any of her earlier fiction.

In "Before Breakfast," too, written at nearly the same time as "The Best Years," Cather further cements her ties with both the Northeast and with the need for a quiet domestic center. Facing age and death, after the loss of nearly everyone she had loved but also after a life's search for meaning and achievement, Cather could turn directly in this late story to questions she had first posed twenty years before. There she could find, in describing her Grand Manan home, a regeneration to answer the blackness of two of her darkest works, *My Mortal Enemy* and *The Professor's House*. Like Godfrey St-Peter, Henry Grenfell, no longer young, and beginning to question the worth of the things for which he had sacrificed his strength, faces the emptiness of his soul.

> What a dreadful night! The speeds which machinists had worked up in the past fifty years were mere baby-talk to what can go through a man's head between dusk and daybreak. In the last ten hours poor Grenfell had travelled over seas and continents, gone through boyhood and youth, founded a business, made a great deal of money, and brought up an expensive family. There were three sons, to whom he had given every advantage and who had turned out well, two of them brilliantly. And all of this meant nothing to him except negatively—"to avoid worse rape," he quoted Milton to himself. (OB, 149)

Again like Godfrey St-Peter, who trembles at his distorted dreams of his own daughters, Grenfell regards his sons with fear and from a sense of isolation.

> But God, they're as cold as ice! I can't see through it. They've never lived at all, those two fellows. They've never run after the ball— they're so damned clever they don't have to. They just reach out and take the ball. Yes, fine hands, like their grandmother's; long ... white ... beautiful nails. ... I'm glad my paws are red and stubby. (OB, 152)

He is further divided from his family by his own demand for privacy, as when he angrily resents his son Harrison's familiarity and reflects that he "never bothered his family with his personal diversions, and he never intruded upon theirs" (OB, 154). And, resembling St-Peter as well as the even more tormented Myra Henshawe, Grenfell also expresses disillusionment over the changed relationship with his spouse, who is as foreign to him as are his sons. "When he thought everything over, here in this great quiet, in this great darkness, he admitted that his shipwreck had not been on the family rock. The bitter truth was that his worst enemy was closer even than the wife of his bosom—was his bosom itself!" (OB, 156)

In "Before Breakfast," however, Cather does not let her protagonist suffer under the power of the science that so disturbs Godfrey St-Peter, or of the personal alienation that threatens both St-Peter's and Myra Henshawe's very souls. For Grenfell, as for Father Latour in *Death Comes for the Archbishop*, revelation comes with a thawing of troubled thoughts and the sense of belonging to something greater than his own constricted world or troubled private family. Grenfell's merging into a larger order is prompted by the eternal grandeurs and the verities they represent in "the quiet centre" of Cather's own northeastern home, a home even dearer to her since the loss of her parents and her discovery of the enduring culture of Quebec.

In words reminiscent of Latour's joy as he returns to New Mexico and its "something soft and wild and free, something that . . . lightened the heart, softly . . . picked the lock, slid the bolts, and released the prisoned spirit of man,"[29] Grenfell finds relief in his own Northeast retreat, where he muses:

> Last night had been one of those nights of revelation, revaluation, when everything seems to come clear. In a low cabin on a high red cliff over-hanging the sea, everything that was shut up in him, under lock and bolt and pressure, simply broke jail, spread out into the spaciousness of night, undraped, unashamed. (OB, 149)

Grenfell finds this release among the beautiful natural images Cather, too, so admired. Climbing a trail on his island retreat, "like Christian of old, he thought, he had left his burden at the bottom of the hill" (OB, 162). In the face of his surroundings, Grenfell, like the aged but reconciled Latour, also comes to realize that "nothing had changed. Everything was the same, and he, Henry Grenfell, was the same: the relationship was unchanged" (OB, 162).

Recognizing the symbolic meaning that resides in the most ordinary things, in this story as in past works, Cather turned to the romantic imagination for the saving grace it could offer her protagonist;[30] that is, she imbues natural phenomena with symbolic meaning so that Grenfell finds comfort in the Grandfather tree, based on an actual fallen spruce that Cather often visited on Grand Manan,[31] and in the morning star, which Grenfell realizes with satisfaction is many times older than the 136 million years a visiting geologist has given as the age of his island. In this story of his restorative isolation on Grand Manan, Grenfell directly addresses both the morning star and the ancient tree. "'Hello, Grandfather!'" (OB, 160) he says appreciatively as he attempts to snap a twig from a branch, just as he calls out as if in complicity, "'And what's a hundred and thirty-six million years to you, Madam?'" to the morning star (OB, 144). In both natural symbols, Grenfell, himself feeling old and cast off, seeks the comfort of agelessness.

It is in neither the spruce nor the glimmering planet, however, that Grenfell finds his greatest solace. In a splendid twist of irony, Cather chooses yet another natural phenomenon, the human offspring of the very geologist whose pronouncements have so unnerved Grenfell, as the vehicle for her protagonist's final epiphany of belonging. Watching the young woman about to take an early morning swim in the frigid north Atlantic waters, Grenfell is at first filled with dread, then with admiration for her, as he reluctantly acknowledges the place of her humanity, and thus his own, as one with the eternity of the morning star or the staunchest forest giant. "She hadn't dodged," he remarks. "She had gone out, and she had come back. She would have a happy day. He knew just how she felt" (OB, 165–66).

In these realizations, Grenfell has moved from his first comparison between the young woman in her pink bathing suit and one of the earliest forms of life, a clam, to his witnessing of her triumph in the face of the vast Atlantic. Admitting that "plucky youth is more bracing than enduring age," and for the first time on this visit finding that "everything since he left the cabin had been reassuring, delightful" (OB, 166), Grenfell can turn from nonhuman natural symbols to the warmth of a young woman and conclude, "'Anyhow, when that first amphibious frog-toad found his water-hole dried up behind him, and jumped out to hop along till he could find another—well, he started on a long hop'" (OB, 166). Cather underscores Grenfell's new sense of hopefulness by her careful use of domestic detail in describing his haste and heightened appetite as he returns to his cabin for breakfast, and in his renewed sense of humor as he chuckles to himself over what he has just seen. The sense of security Grenfell has earlier lost in his private home is restored, as he forgets the "first sleepless night he had ever spent in his own cabin, on his own island" (OB, 141) and awakens to the present reality of "wood smoke rising from the chimney" and savors "the smell of coffee [that] drowned the spruce smell and sea smells" (OB, 166)

In relating Grenfell's final insights and admission, Cather reconciles him to personal death as her famous professor is never reconciled, just as she gives him a more comforting interpretation of a scientific principle, evolution, than Godfrey St-Peter achieves.[32] Grenfell also earns a sense of affirmation that is at best problematic for a character like Myra Henshawe.[33] What he senses as he gazes at the youthful swimmer and at the ocean from his forest walk is what, in her earlier works, Cather expressed as the fate of faithful hearts, like Alexandra Bergson's, that die only to be given "out again in the yellow wheat, in the rustling corn, in the shining eyes of youth!"[34] In the years between her earliest and latest stories, two world wars and the deaths of nearly all those she loved intervened. But for Willa Cather, the one thread that held these diverse works together was finding her own center of life and art, a sense of balance and peace achieved for the artist, as for her famous Count Frontenac, after a lifelong struggle for "individual achievement" and "distinctive activity," followed by an equally urgent search for belonging and "attachment."[35] This gift of connection, an inheritance from mentors like Sarah Orne Jewett which Cather's own perseverance allowed to grow, remained with her as she moved from youth to age, and from the diverse places she seems paradoxically to have considered as home.

That she chose for her final resting place a plot in Jaffrey

Center, New Hampshire, with a view of Mt. Monadnock, and that it is here she wished to rest under the inscription, That Is Happiness; to Be Dissolved into Something Complete and Great, is perhaps her finest tribute to the region where her heart most truly took its rest. It also bears witness to her finding as great a sense of belonging in the Northeast, with its fine sense of harmony and domestic order, as in any place she had known since the Virginia of her earliest childhood.

Notes

Chapter 1. Cather's Literary and Personal Search

1. Sarah Orne Jewett, *The Letters of Sarah Orne Jewett*, ed. Richard Cary (Waterville, Maine: Colby College Press, 1967), 250.

2. The interview cited was taken from the *Philadelphia Record*, 10 Aug. 1913, as cited by L. Brent Bohlke in *Willa Cather in Person* (Lincoln and London: University of Nebraska Press, 1986), 10.

3. James Woodress's full mention of the dichotomy between Nebraska and the East follows:

> Among the several dichotomies in her life, this is one. Throughout her life she was drawn back to the hills and mountains [recalling her earliest Virginia home] despite her acquired affection for the prairie. When she discovered Jaffrey, New Hampshire, in 1916, she immediately fell in love with the area and returned year after year for a month or more; and when she died, she was not buried in the family plot at Red Cloud with her parents, but on a hillside at Jaffrey, where one could look up and see "a familiar mountain" (Monadnock) against the sky. [Woodress, *Willa Cather, A Literary Life* (Lincoln and London: University of Nebraska Press, 1987, 37]

4. Ibid., 112.

5. Edith Lewis, *Willa Cather Living: A Personal Record* (1953; reprint, Lincoln and London: University of Nebraska Press, 1976), 104–5.

6. Ibid., 129, 130.

7. Ibid., 153.

8. E. K. Brown and Leon Edel, *Willa Cather: A Critical Biography* (1953; reprint, Lincoln and London: University of Nebraska Press, 1987), 288.

9. Willa Cather, *Not Under Forty* (1936; reprint, Lincoln and London: University of Nebraska Press, 1988), 57.

10. Sharon O'Brien, *Willa Cather: The Emerging Voice* (New York: Oxford University Press, 1987), 318.

11. Cather wrote this in a letter to DeWolfe Howe, dated 11 December 1931. The original is in the Houghton Library, Harvard University.

12. Lewis, *Willa Cather Living*, 151, 153.

13. John J. Murphy, "*Shadows on the Rock*: Cather's Medieval Refuge," *Renascence* 15 (Winter 1963): 78.

14. L. Brent Bohlke, ed., *Willa Cather in Person* (Lincoln and London: University of Nebraska Press, 1986), 71.

15. Ibid., 114–15.

16. Willa Cather, *Willa Cather on Writing* (1920; reprint, Lincoln and London: University of Nebraska Press, 1988), 16.

17. Lewis, *Willa Cather Living*, 88–89.

18. Cather wrote this letter to Zoe Akins on 20 April 1922. The original is in the Huntington Library, San Marino, California.

19. Hermione Lee, *Willa Cather: Double Lives* (New York: Pantheon, 1989), 293.

20. Woodress, *Literary Life*, 426.

21. Robert J. Nelson, *Willa Cather and France: In Search of the Lost Language* (Urbana and Chicago: University of Illinois Press, 1988), 68.

22. Jewett, *Letters of Sarah Orne Jewett*, 247–50.

23. O'Brien, *Willa Cather*, 28.

24. Ibid., 29. O'Brien underscores a maturing Cather's agreement with Jewett's emphasis on domesticity as art by citing Cather's fascination with Jewett's "Martha's Lady." This fascination, to O'Brien, is a possible "intense response to [Cather's] . . . identification with Martha, the clumsy maid who learns housekeeping skills from Helena [Jewett]." O'Brien extends the comparison, seeing Helena's "passing on the traditions of flower-arranging and food preparation . . . [as] a 'gift from heart to heart'" and Helena herself as "both the model and the imagined audience for Martha's creativity—the reader of the texts she creates in table settings and flower arrangements" (34).

25. Ibid., 332.

26. Ibid., 341.

27. Josephine Donovan, in her *New England Local Color Literature: Women's Tradition* (New York: Ungar, 1983), describes in detail the importance of antiindustrial sentiments and the establishment of "a supportive community of women, sutained by a kind of matriarchal Christianity, and by traditions of women's lore and culture" to local color literature (103ff.).

28. Helen Fiddyment Levy, *Fiction of the Home Place* (Jackson and London: University Press of Mississippi, 1992), 4.

29. Ibid., 24.

30. Donovan, *New England Local Color Literature*, 102–3.

31. Brown and Edel, *Willa Cather*, 139–40.

32. Donovan, *New England Local Color Literature*, 107. In *The Voyage Perilous: Willa Cather's Romanticism* (Lincoln and London: University of Nebraska Press, 1986), Susan J. Rosowski defines the term *romanticism* as

> a historical movement that in literature began in the late eighteenth century in reaction against dehumanizing implications of the scientific world view. The essential characteristic of romanticism concerns a mode of perception by which the imagination is used in its synthesizing or creating powers to transform and give meaning to an alien or meaningless material world . . . both [moderns and Romantics] look to the individual creative imagination to create a new order. (X)

Merrill Maguire Skaggs, in her *After the World Broke in Two: The Later Novels of Willa Cather* (Charlottesville and London: The University Press of Virginia, 1990), also describes the effect of imaginatively realistic writing, though without using the term *imaginative realism*. To Skaggs, Cather's works, taken together, seem to be "as centrally concerned with capturing light and motion as do the canvasses of the French Impressionists she loved" (21). Both Cather's fiction, particularly *Shadows*, and Impressionist art blend representational realism and Romantic suggestion.

33. Donovan, *New England Local Color Literature*, 12.

34. Ibid., 99. Donovan's more detailed explanation of Jewett's advances over other local colorists states that Jewett went beyond her peers to the creation of

an authentically female-identified vision of her own ... a woman's vision of transcendence ... no longer one of naive optimism ... [but a] recognition of the troubles
that concern the late Phelps and Freeman—anxiety over an encroaching male domination, the "burglars in paradise." With Jewett, neither the anxieties nor the burglar
prevail. The encroachment is resisted, the female sanctuary preserved.... Jewett
was able to transcend this impasse [blocking of women's fulfillment by patriarchal
domination in the 1880s] by establishing a vision of a supportive community of
women, sustained by a kind of matriarchal Christianity, and by traditions of
women's lore and culture. (99)

35. Ibid., 103.

36. Ibid., 115.

37. Margaret Roman, *Sarah Orne Jewett: Reconstructing Gender* (Tuscaloosa and London: The University of Alabama Press, 1992), 221.

38. Rosowski gives a more detailed discussion of the Marian structure of
Shadows in *The Voyage Perilous*, chap. 12, 184–87.

39. Cather, *Willa Cather on Writing*, 16.

40. Rosowski, *Voyage Perilous*, 178.

41. Fiddyment Levy, *Fiction of the Home Place*, 7, 9–10.

42. Skaggs, *After the World Broke in Two*, 131.

43. Roman, *Sarah Orne Jewett*, 155.

44. Rosowksi, *Voyage Perilous*, 179.

45. Sarah Orne Jewett, *The Country of the Pointed Firs and Other Stories*
(1896; reprint, Garden City, N.Y.: Doubleday Anchor Books, 1956), 58.

46. Others also describe narrative voices and patterns of storytelling
shared by Cather and Jewett. Fiddyment Levy, in *Fiction of the Home Place*,
considers Rachel Blau Du Plessis's "formulation [in which] women poets
reshape ritualistic, religious, and legendary materials, as the voice of
women's communities overcomes the individualistic language of the father"
(23). In discussing Jewett's *Country of the Pointed Firs* in particular, Fiddyment Levy further notes how the narrator "must seek to join her national
culture through use of the associational language, but at the same time she
must try to evoke the communal language ... [and partake] of a double
cultural experience" (56). Ann Romines, in *The Home Plot: Women, Writing
and Domestic Ritual* (Amherst: University of Massachusetts Press, 1992),
places Cather and Jewett in an even more established narrative tradition
stating that, at about the time of the Civil War, American women writers
began to treat domestic artists and housekeeping "in a new way ... as subject and ongoing substance ... some of the best fiction by American women
writers is dominated and shaped by the rhythms and stresses of domestic
ritual" (9). She goes on to define "the poetics of domestic ritual" as character-
ized by "regular recurrences, symbolic value, emotional meaning, and (usually) a 'dramatic' group-making quality" (12). Of *Country of the Pointed Firs*
itself, Romines concludes, "Its greatness is not as a final, accomplished prod-
uct, but ... as a richly ambiguous process of repetitive, continuing work,
spelled out in women's changing lives" (90).

47. Cather, *Shadows on the Rock* (1931; reprint, New York: Vintage Books,
1971), 36–37. Subsequent references are to this edition.

48. O'Brien, *Willa Cather*, 340. See also Rosowski, *Voyage Perilous*, 179.

49. Rosowski, *Voyage Perilous*, 184.

50. Ibid., 185–86.

51. O'Brien, *Willa Cather*, 28.

52. Romines, *Home Plot*, 152.

53. Ibid., 163.

54. Cather, *My Ántonia* (1918; reprint, Boston: Houghton, 1977), 352.

55. David Stouck, *Willa Cather's Imagination* (Lincoln and London: University of Nebraska Press, 1975), 119. Stouck draws other distinctions between *Death Comes for the Archbishop* and *Shadows*. Despite acknowledging a healing tone in the later novel, Stouck views *Shadows* as greatly influenced by Cather's personal losses at the time of her writing of the novel—the death of her father and illness of her mother, and her dislocation from her established apartment. As a result, he finds the novel "obsessed with life's vicissitudes and the fact of man's mortality" (119) and a statement of "the author's personal purgatory" (120).

56. Although Cather's domestic vision remains uniquely her own, her fictive worlds share many common elements with those of Jewett and other women writers. In *Fiction of the Home Place*, Fiddyment Levy views familial and matriarchal connections as powerful enough to form, in the case of an accomplished domestic artist like Mrs. Blackett in *Country of the Pointed Firs*, "the spiritual and bodily source of Dunnet Landing, and by extension, America, [as] appears in the climax of the narrative, the Bowden reunion" (60). She adds, in language that could as aptly describe Cécile Auclair and her domestic haven in *Shadows*, "the home place would refuse the injustice of the paternalistic community as well as the oppression of the material competition of the social structure," thus making of the "seer" or domestic artist's home a shelter for "all who seek its protection . . . a consciously imaginary social order, based in the memory of female family and friendships" (226).

Chapter 2. The Early Fiction, Its Connection to Cather's Life, and the Beginnings of *Shadows on the Rock*

1. Merrill Maguire Skaggs, *After the World Broke in Two: The Later Novels of Willa Cather* (Charlottesville and London: The University Press of Virginia, 1990), ix.

2. Willa Cather, *Alexander's Bridge* (1912; reprint, Lincoln and London: University of Nebraska Press, 1977), 114. Subsequent references are to this edition, abbreviated AB.

3. Bernice Slote, ed., *The Kingdom of Art: Willa Cather's First Principles and Critical Statements, 1893–1896* (Lincoln and London: University of Nebraska Press, 1966), 449.

4. Ibid., 448.

5. Cather, *Willa Cather on Writing* (1920; reprint, Lincoln and London: University of Nebraska Press, 1988), 92–94.

6. Slote, *Kingdom of Art*, 447.

7. The letter to Jewett is dated 24 October 1908. The original is in the Houghton Library, Harvard University.

8. James Woodress, *Willa Cather, A Literary Life* (Lincoln and London: University of Nebraska Press, 1987), 205.

9. Virginia Faulkner, ed., *Willa Cather's Collected Short Fiction, 1892–1912* (Lincoln and London: University of Nebraska Press, 1965), 2. Subsequent references are to this edition, abbreviated CSF.

10. Despite earlier praise for domestic touches that are overlooked in *Alexander's Bridge*, a comparison of the feasts and culinary artistry in "The Bohemian Girl" and *Alexander's Bridge* makes clear the relative lack of domestic detail in Cather's first novel. In contrast to Johanna Vavrika's vast array of food described in "The Bohemian Girl" is the "wonderful little dinner" Bartley Alexander enjoys at Hilda Burgoyne's apartment: "watercress soup, and sole, and a delightful omelette stuffed with mushrooms and truffles, and two small rare ducklings, and artichokes, and a dry yellow Rhone wine" (52). The meals are as different in quantity and robustness as they are in their preparation and in the home-grown origin of Johanna Vavrika's offerings.

11. Sharon O'Brien, *Willa Cather: The Emerging Voice* (New York: Oxford University Press, 1987), 348.

12. Cather, *O Pioneers!* (1913; reprint, Boston: Houghton, 1941), 309. Subsequent references are to this edition, abbreviated OP.

13. Cather, *My Ántonia* (1918; reprint, Boston: Houghton, 1977), 339. Subsequent references are to this edition, abbreviated MA.

14. Cather, *One of Ours* (1922; reprint, New York: Vintage Books, 1971), 390.

15. Cather, *A Lost Lady* (1923; reprint, New York: Vintage Books, 1972), 152.

16. Cather, *My Mortal Enemy* (1926; reprint, New York: Vintage Books, 1954), 11, 26.

17. Ibid., 57.

18. Cather, *Death Comes for the Archbishop* (1927; reprint, New York: Vintage Books, 1971), 38–39. Subsequent references are to this edition, abbreviated DCA.

19. Edith Lewis, *Willa Cather Living: A Personal Record* (1953; reprint, Lincoln and London: University of Nebraska Press, 1976), 157.

20. Woodress, *Willa Cather*, 414.

21. Lewis, *Willa Cather Living*, 153.

22. Ibid., 157.

23. Edward A. and Lillian D. Bloom, "*Shadows on the Rock:* Notes on the Composition of a Novel," *Twentieth Century Literature* 2 (July 1956): 78, 80–81.

24. Ibid., 83.

25. Francis Parkman, *The Struggle for a Continent*, ed. Pelham Edgar (Boston: Little, Brown, 1907), 155.

26. Parkman, *Count Frontenac and New France Under Louis XIV*, pt. 5 of *France and England in North America* (Boston: Little, Brown, 1897), 175.

27. Quebec fell to the English on 13 September 1759, with the decisive victory of the British general James Wolfe over Gen. Louis Joseph Montcalm, on Quebec's historic Plains of Abraham. The thoroughness of the French defeat suggests that Montcalm was, indeed, not a man of Frontenac's ability, though both the victorious General Wolfe and Montcalm died in the battle.

28. Among the marvels Parkman credits to the Jesuits are burying "themselves in deserts, facing death with the courage of heroes, and enduring torments with the constancy of martyrs." He describes them "among the frozen forests of Acadia, struggling on snow-shoes with some wandering Algonquin horde, or crouching in the crowded hunting-lodge, half stifled in the smoky den, and battling with troops of famished dogs for the last morsel of sustenance." Of their courage he writes that the Jesuit took "his life in his hand, carr[ying] his sacred mission into the strongholds of the Iroquois, like

one who invades unarmed a den of angry tigers" (*Struggle for a Continent*, 130–31). Ultimately, however, Parkman concludes that "not a vestige of early Jesuit influence can be found among the tribes" and "the seed was sown upon a rock" (133).

29. Cather, *Shadows on the Rock* (1931; reprint, New York: Vintage Books, 1971), 136–37. Subsequent references are to this edition, abbreviated SOR.

30. Ann Romines, "The Hermit's Parish: Jeanne Le Ber and Cather's Legacy from Jewett," *Cather Studies* 1 (1990): 152.

31. Hermione Lee, *Willa Cather: Double Lives* (New York: Pantheon, 1989), 305.

32. Étienne Faillon, *The Christian Heroine of Canada; or, Life of Miss LeBer* (Montreal: John Lovell, 1861), 63.

33. Ibid., 69.

34. Ibid., 71.

35. Ibid., 73.

36. Ibid., 129.

37. Ibid., 123–24.

38. Paul Ragueneau's text, with original spelling and punctuation retained, follows:

Peu apres le coeur de Monsieur du Longpré son père se trouva heuresement changé: Nôtre Seigneur permit que ce bon Gentilhomme étant tombé malade de chagrin et de melancolie à cette occasion, demanda à voir une Relation nouvellement venue du Canada, qui parlait de la mort du Père Isaac Jogues Jesuite, massacré par les Iroquois l'année d'auparavant 1647, lors qu'il était allé pour la troisième fois dans leur pais, pour leur porter la Foy de JESUS-CHRIST. Ce père abbatu de tristesse, fut saisi tout d'un coup d'un assoupissement et d'un sommeil, sans doute mysterieux; pendant lequel il fut inspiré et porté fortement de permettre à notre Catherine de faire ce grand voyage; et Mademoiselle sa mere en meme temps eut aussi la meme pensée, quoy qu'elle fut éloignée pour lors de son mary. A son reveil son coeur se sentit tout changé sur ce genereux sacrifice que voulait faire sa fille d'elle-meme; et il conçut une si vive apprehension que Dieu ne luy demandat compte à l'heure de la mort, de l'opposition si opiniatre qu'il faisait a ses volontez, et aux desseins que le Ciel avait sur sa fille, que touché de cette pensée qui le pressait fortement; il accorda à Dieu ce qu'il avait refusè aux hommes. [Ragueneau, *La vie de la Mère Catherine de Saint Augustin* (1671; reprint, 1923, Quebec: Hôtel-Dieu de Qúebec, 1923), 36]

39. Ragueneau's text follows:

Elle était aimée de tous ceux qu'elle connaissait et qu'elle allait quitter . . . la Communauté des Religieuses de Bayeux oú elle avait deux soeurs, sa grand'mère, et une tante soeur de sa grand'mère, et une cousine germaine Fondatrice de cette Maison, et où toutes les autres Religieuses la portaient dans leur coeur, et pour lesquelles elle avait des tendresses inimaginables; toute cette chere Communauté luy causa au point de sa separation une douleur plus sensible qu'elle ne le pouvait exprimer. (Ibid., 38)

40. Ragueneau's text follows: "Hélas! sainte Vierge Marie, je suis indigne de porter vôtre nom; mais je vous prie ne souffrir pas que je sois damnée. Je vous en prie pour la consideration de ce nom." (Ibid., 188)

41. Ragueneau's original sentence from which these words are taken follows: "Plus de vingt ans avant sa mort elle n'avait eu recours aucun ni à Dieu, ni à la Sainte Vierge, ny aux Saints. Elle avait quitté les Sacramens, et tout le respect qu'elle avait aux choses saintes. . . ." (Ibid., 188).

42. Ragueneau's original text follows:

Dieu prit souvent cette voye de conduite avec elle, qu'elle était comme une prison à plusieurs milliers de démons, qui se voyaient contraints, malgré toutes leurs resistances, d'entrer dans cette fille vrayement Sainte, dont ils avaient plus d'horreur que de l'enfer même: Car plus ils exerçaient contr'elle toute leur rage, par toutes sortes de tentations dont les impressions étaient extremes; toujours ces maudits esprits d'enfer se voyaient vaincus par cette ame, qui était si fidele à la grace de JESUS-CHRIST, que jamais ils n'ont pu obtenir d'elle qu'elle consentit à la moindre chose qui'lls desiraient. . . . En sorte que bien loin de la posseder ils etaient eux-memes captifs en elle; et ne pouvaient agir sur d'autres que sur elle; et souvent le nombre en a ètè si grand et si excessif, dont elle sentait les impressions, que cette pauvre fille avait à combattre des armées entieres de démons. (Ibid., 109)

43. Ragueneau's text follows:

Ce fut à ce grand serviteur de Dieu, à ce grand Homme Apostolique, à ce premier Apôtre des Hurons, que JESUS-CHRIST confia le soin de sa fidele servante et épouse, pour la proteger puissamment contre toutes les attaques et embûches des démons, et afin de luy servir de Directeur et Conducteur, dans un chemin si difficile et si dangereux, par où la divine Providence la vouloit conduire à une haute sainteté. (Ibid., 114)

44. Jeanne Franc de la Ferté Saint-Ignace, Mère Juschereau, *Les annales de l'Hôtel-Dieu de Québec* (Québec: Hôtel-Dieu de Québec, 1939), 422.

Chapter 3. *Shadows on the Rock* and Cather's Interpretation of the History of New France

1. Willa Cather, *Shadows on the Rock* (1931; reprint, New York: Vintage Books, 1971), 157–58.
2. Sarah Orne Jewett, *The Country of the Pointed Firs and Other Stories* (1896; reprint, Garden City, N.Y.: Doubleday Anchor Books, 1957), 52.
3. Hermione Lee, *Willa Cather: Double Lives* (New York: Pantheon Books, 1989), 292.
4. Ibid., 303.
5. Francis Parkman, *The Struggle for a Continent*, ed. Pelham Edgar (Boston: Little, Brown, 1907), 130.
6. Ibid., 224–25.
7. Ibid., *Count Frontenac and New France Under Louis XIV*, pt. 5 of *France and England in North America* (Boston: Little, Brown, 1897), 71.
8. Parkman, *Struggle for a Continent*, 225.
9. Ibid., 224.
10. Parkman, *Count Frontenac*, 2:53.
11. Edward A. and Lillian D. Bloom, "*Shadows on the Rock:* Notes on the Composition of a Novel," *Twentieth Century Literature* 2 (July 1956): 78.
12. Adrien Leblond De Brumath, *Bishop Laval*, in *The Makers of Canada* (Toronto: Morang & Co., 1910), 253, 255.
13. Abbé Henri A. Scott, *Bishop Laval*, in *The Makers of Canada*, Anniversary Edition (Toronto: Oxford University Press, 1926), 316.
14. Ann Romines, *The Home Plot: Women, Writing and Domestic Ritual* (Amherst: University of Massachusetts Press, 1992), 166.

15. Cather, *Obscure Destinies* (1932; reprint, New York: Vintage Books, 1974), 93.

16. Romines, *Home Plot*, 167.

17. Cather's merging of gender roles in her depictions of male heroes will be considered in greater detail later in this chapter, especially in the section when she alters the historical attributes of Count Frontenac. Such characteristics will be discussed in terms of gender-specific behavior, as defined by the developmental theorist Carol Gilligan. Gilligan's work will also be cited in chap. 5, on the further connection between Cather's and Jewett's characterization and structure.

18. De Brumath, *Bishop Laval*, 249, 255.

19. Ibid., 257–58.

20. Ibid., 258.

21. Scott, *Bishop Laval*, 315–16.

22. Helen Fiddyment Levy, *Fiction of the Home Place* (Jackson, Miss. and London: University Press of Mississippi, 1992), 8.

23. Ibid., 75, 92.

24. Merrill Maguire Skaggs, *After the World Broke in Two: The Later Novels of Willa Cather* (Charlottesville and London: The University Press of Virginia, 1990), 131.

25. Ibid., 132, 139.

26. Carol Gilligan, *In a Different Voice* (Cambridge: Harvard University Press, 1982), 163–64.

27. Ibid., 164–65, 167–68.

28. Parkman, *Struggle for a Continent*, 255.

29. Parkman, *Count Frontenac*, 1:74.

30. Ibid., 2:29.

31. Ibid., 2:82.

32. Ibid., 1:195–96.

33. Parkman, *Struggle for a Continent*, 226.

34. Reuben Gold Thwaites, ed., *The Jesuit Relations and Allied Documents: Travels and Explorations of the Jesuit Missioniaries in New France, 1610–1791* (Cleveland: The Burrows Brothers Company, 1900), 64:121.

35. Ibid., 64:147.

36. Ibid., 64:123.

Chapter 4. The Central Role of Cécile and Her Domestic Art in *Shadows on the Rock*

1. See Susan J. Rosowski, *The Voyage Perilous: Willa Cather's Romanticism* (Nebraska: University of Nebraska Press, 1986), 184; and Hermione Lee, *Willa Cather: Double Lives* (New York: Pantheon Books, 1989), 304.

2. Ann Romines's interpretation of Jeanne Le Ber and Joanna Todd presents both recluses in a more positive light. Joanna's story, to Romines, is "physically and thematically central to" *The Country of the Pointed Firs* and "initiates a complex meditation, both communal and solitary, on the nature of shelter." She also sees *Shadows* "with its subtly experimental form and its domestic focus" as resembling *The Country of the Pointed Firs* "in many telling ways" ("The Hermit's Parish: Jeanne Le Ber and Cather's Legacy from Jewett," *Cather Studies* 1 [1990]: 90).

For Romines, both characters are alike in having "wills so powerful that they can reshape the patterns their respective societies offer women. They turn their backs on conventional sexual and domestic life" while, through their passion and occupations, both remain "quintessentially domestic. Their meticulously ordered housekeeping is raised to a state of ardent awareness that becomes highly conscious art." By becoming "their own mysterious legends," she adds, both women "paradoxically give themselves to the very communities they left" (91).

This thesis gains support from Jewett's descriptions of the "one thing" Joanna had done "very pretty" in her island cottage, her braiding of rushes into "beautiful mats for the floor and a thick cushion for the long bunk," and her arrangement of her "few dishes on a shelf, and, flowers set about in shells fixed to the walls" (68); and from Cather's descriptions of the beautiful weaving of altar cloths and religious garments by Le Ber. The final assessment of Joanna's cabin by Mrs. Todd, the acknowledged domestic artist of *The Country of the Pointed Firs*, however, as "sort of homelike, though so lonely and poor [that] I couldn't keep the tears out o' my eyes, I felt so sad" (68) adds ambiguity to the portrayal, as the images of Le Ber's sparse and graceless cell raise questions about the degree of refined domestic artistry her life exemplifies.

Much recent criticism also questions the artistry of these reclusive characters, with Margaret Roman in *Sarah Orne Jewett: Reconstructing Gender* (Tuscaloosa, Ala. and London: The University of Alabama Press, 1992) judging that Joanna Todd "embraces deprivation" and "accentuate[s] her folly" by adopting "a narrow, rigid male vision" of Christianity (221). She concludes her discussion of "Poor Joanna" with the assessment that the narrator of *The Country of the Pointed Firs* finally "can not dismiss the poverty of her [Joanna's] choice" (222). In her study, Helen Fiddyment Levy faults such hermits for failing to achieve "the proper balancing of life and eternity" (Fiddyment Levy, *Fiction of the Home Place* [Jackson, Miss. and London: University Press of Mississippi, 1992], 59) and for living a life that is more a precautionary than an exemplary tale. Such a failed domestic artist, to Fiddyment Levy, leaves nothing of her own that is permanent and so ultimately "vanishes into . . . romantic drama" (60).

3. Willa Cather, *Shadows on the Rock* (1931; reprint New York: Vintage Books, 1971), 25. Subsequent references are to this edition, abbreviated SOR.

4. Fiddyment Levy, *Fiction of the Home Place*, 65, 92.

5. Ibid., 92.

6. Ibid., 34, 225.

7. Merrill Maguire Skaggs, *After the World Broke in Two: The Later Novels of Willa Cather* (Charlottesville and London: The University Press of Virginia, 1990), 132.

8. Ibid., 143, 145.

9. Ann Romines, *The Home Plot: Women, Writing and Domestic Ritual* (Amherst: University of Massachusetts Press, 1992), 12.

10. Skaggs, *Later Novels of Willa Cather*, 139.

11. Fiddyment Levy, *Fiction of the Home Place*, 65.

12. Josephine Donovan, *New England Local Color Literature: A Women's Tradition* (New York: Ungar, 1983), 113.

13. See the discussion of "imaginative realism" in chap. 1.

14. See Stephen Vincent and Rosemary Benet's interview of Cather, in the 15 December 1940 *New York Herald Tribune Books*, reprinted in L. Brent

Bohlke's *Willa Cather in Person* (Lincoln and London: University of Nebraska Press, 1986). The Benets write: "She [Cather] has always had a deep feeling for the frontier, for its freshness and strength, for the wild beauty of new land. At the same time she has liked to put a highly cultivated person against that setting" (Bohlke, 137).

15. David Stouck, *Willa Cather's Imagination* (Lincoln and London: University of Nebraska Press, 1975), 120.

16. Cather, *Death Comes for the Archbishop* (1927; reprint, New York: Vintage Books, 1971), 257.

17. Hermione Lee, *Willa Cather: Double Lives* (New York: Pantheon Books, 1989), 304.

18. Donovan, *Women's Tradition*, 103.

19. Elizabeth Ammons, in her "Going in Circles: The Female Geography of Jewett's *Country of the Pointed Firs*" (*Studies in the Literary Imagination* 16 [Fall 1983]: 85) describes Jewett's narrative structure in these terms. In the same passage, Ammons also praises the networked and webbed plot structure as being "inclusive and accumulative [rather than relationally exclusive]: relationships do not vie with but complement each other."

20. Ibid., 84.

21. The climate Cécile helps create in New France is no less than the domestic center achieved by Jewett's Mrs. Blackett, even in the old woman's apotheosis as she reigns over the Bowden family reunion in *The Country of the Pointed Firs*. The importance of the reunion is great enough to be considered by Fiddyment Levy as "the matrix, the creative source, of the American nation, from which all the male adventurers journey forth and to which they will return in life or in death" (Fiddyment Levy, *Fiction of the Home Place*, 48). Fiddyment Levy views Mrs. Blackett as so central to Jewett's world as to become not only "the spiritual and bodily source of Dunnet Landing" but also, "by extension, [of] America, [as] appears in the climax of the narrative, the Bowden reunion" (60). By the end of *Shadows*, the same procreative power might well be attributed to Cécile, who has succeeded in making a home for her coureur-de-bois husband Pierre Charron, in raising four sons, and in continuing to nurture her aging father and the traditions he symbolizes.

22. Beverly Gail Busch, *The Nature and Extent of the Influence of Sarah Orne Jewett on Willa Sibert Cather* (Ph.D. diss., Drew University, Madison, N.J. (Ann Arbor: UMI, 1986, 8616862), 45.

23. Sarah Orne Jewett, *The Country of the Pointed Firs and Other Stories* (1896; reprint, Garden City, N. Y.: Doubleday Anchor Books, 1956), 48. Subsequent references are to this edition, abbreviated CPF.

24. Cather, *My Ántonia* (1918; reprint; Boston: Houghton, 1977), 7, 8.

25. CPF, ii.

Chapter 5. Cather's Inheritance—and Sense of Peace— In Her Last Works

1. Letter to Viola Roseboro on the writing of *Sapphira and the Slave Girl*, 9 November 1940. The original is in the University of Virginia Library.

2. Willa Cather, *Obscure Destinies* (1932; reprint, New York: Vintage Books, 1974), 219. Subsequent references are to this edition, abbreviated OD.

3. Ann Romines, *The Home Plot: Women, Writing and Domestic Ritual* (Amherst: University of Massachusetts Press, 1992), 152.

4. Cather, *Lucy Gayheart* (1935; reprint, New York: Vintage Books, 1976), 156. Subsequent references are to this edition, abbreviated LG.

5. Merrill Maguire Skaggs asserts in *After the World Broke in Two: The Later Novels of Willa Cather* (Charlottesville and London: The University Press of Virginia, 1990), that any lasting emotional energy in *Lucy Gayheart* comes from Harry Gordon. In him, Skaggs, argues, Cather celebrates a sense of survival and mature seasoning (162). In fact, at core, to Skaggs, this is a novel of forgiveness in which ego is set aside, so that, in art and life, those who have caused pain are forgiven. Skaggs suggests that writing this novel late in her life may have been Cather's expression of forgiveness for Isabelle McClung when she compromised the closeness of her and Cather's relationship through her marriage, for example.

6. James Woodress, *Willa Cather, A Literary Life* (Lincoln and London: University of Nebraska Press, 1987), 478, 479.

7. Ibid., 479.

8. Ibid., 480.

9. Cather, *Sapphira and the Slave Girl* (1940; reprint; New York: Vintage Books, 1968), 119. Subsequent references are to this edition, abbreviated SSG.

10. Bernice Slote, ed., *The Kingdom of Art: Willa Cather's First Principles and Critical Statements, 1893–1896* (Lincoln and London: University of Nebraska Press, 1966), 449.

11. Sarah Orne Jewett, *The Country of the Pointed Firs and Other Stories*, preface by Willa Cather (Garden City, N.Y.: Doubleday Anchor Books, 1956), 7.

12. Elizabeth Ammons, in describing the webbed and circular female geography of Jewett's *Country of the Pointed Firs*, calls the scene between the narrator and Mrs. Todd set in the pennyroyal "the dramatic core of Jewett's narrative, which instead of being climactic might be described as concentric, even vortical." To Ammons, the "emotional energy of the book collects most intensely" in this scene, "from which, in every direction, like rings spreading out when a stone is dropped in a pool, emanates Jewett's drama of female love, which is noncombative and nonlinear." She concludes that "Where Pennyroyal Grew," in its "reproduction of basic female mythic material, holds the book together dramatically and emotionally." (This information comes from Ammons's essay, "Going in Circles: The Female Geography of Jewett's *Country of the Pointed Firs*," *Studies in the Literary Imagination* 16 [Fall 1983]: 91.)

13. Ibid.

14. Ibid.

15. Cather, *Not Under Forty* (1936; reprint, Lincoln and London: University of Nebraska Press, 1988), 57.

16. Beverly Gail Busch (*The Nature and Extent of Influence of Sarah Orne Jewett on Willa Sibert Cather* [Ph.D. diss., Drew University Press, Madison, N.J., 1986. Ann Arbor: VMI. 8616862]) finds the connection between Cather and Jewett even more powerful, with Cather's final peace or finding of her spiritual center coming only after the writing of *Sapphira and the Slave Girl*. Busch writes:

Moving from *O Pioneers!* and *My Ántonia* where there are sections of enlightenment to *Death Comes for the Archbishop* where Cather synthesizes apparently disparate elements, to "Neighbour Rosicky" where, I believe, both theme and style most nearly approach Jewett's own, and concluding with her child-self in *Sapphira and the Slave Girl*, Cather ultimately finds the "quiet centre" she sought. The richness of her art results in large part from her search based in Jewett as a role model. It continued in love for her as an "ideal reader." (169)

17. Romines, *Home Plot*, 185.
18. Ibid., 187.
19. Ibid, 179.
20. Woodress, *Willa Cather*, 476.
21. Cather, *The Old Beauty and Others* (1948; reprint, New York: Vintage Books, 1976), 5. Subsequent references are to this edition, abbreviated OB.
22. Woodress, *Willa Cather*, 475.
23. Ibid., 500.
24. Ibid.
25. Ibid., 501.
26. Ibid.
27. Elizabeth Shepley Sergeant, *Willa Cather: A Memoir* (1953; reprint, Lincoln and London: University of Nebraska Press, 1963), 139.
28. Cather, *My Ántonia* (1918; reprint, Boston: Houghton, 1977), 372.
29. Cather, *Death Comes for the Archbishop* (1927; reprint, New York: Vintage Books, 1971), 276.
30. Susan J. Rosowski's *Voyage Perilous: Willa Cather's Romanticism* (Lincoln and London: University of Nebraska Press, 1986) offers the most in-depth treatment of Cather's use of the romantic imagination. Also see n. 32, Chap. 1.
31. Marion Marsh Brown and Ruth Crone, *Only One Point of the Compass: Willa Cather in the Northeast* (Danbury, Conn.: Archer Editions Press, 1980), 89.
32. St.-Peter's continuing struggle against the scientific advances of modern times is most evident in lines like these, from chap. 5 of *The Professor's House:*

> I don't myself think much of science as a phase of human development. It has given us a lot of ingenious toys; they take our attention away from the real problem. . . . Science hasn't given us any new amazements, except of the superficial kind we get from witnessing dexterity and sleight-of-hand. . . . I don't think you help people by making their conduct of no importance—you impoverish them. As long as every man and woman who crowded into the cathedrals on Easter Sunday was a principal in a gorgeous drama with God, glittering angels on one side and the shadows of evil coming and going on the other, life was a rich thing. . . . Art and religion (they are the same thing, in the end, of course) have given man the only happiness he has ever had. (67–69)

Similarly, his continued reluctance to accept age and death is suggested in his incomplete resolutions in the novel's closing pages. "He had never learned to live without delight," the professor muses.

> And he would have to learn to, just as, in a Prohibition country, he supposed he would have to learn to live without sherry. Theoretically, he knew that life is possible, may be even pleasant, without joy, without passionate griefs. But it had never occurred to him that he might have to live like that. (282)

33. Myra Henshawe is most remembered for her embittered words, "Why must I die like this, alone with my mortal enemy!'" (105). Although the narrator of Myra's story initially finds comfort in her dying on a headland, overlooking the sea, and in the forgiving light of dawn, *My Mortal Enemy* ends with a note of foreboding similar to the fate of Hawthorne's Young Goodman Brown, whose "dying hour was gloom" (Nathaniel Hawthorne, *Selected Short Stories*, ed. Alfred Kazin [Greenwich, Conn.: Fawcett Publications, 1966], 112). That is, when Nellie tries to wear an amethyst necklace Oswald has given her after Myra's death, she feels "a chill over [her] heart" and, despite herself, hears "again that strange complaint breathed by a dying woman into the stillness of night, like a confession of the soul. 'Why must I die like this, alone with my mortal enemy!'" (Willa Cather, *My Mortal Enemy* [1926; reprint, New York: Vintage Books, 1954], 104–5).

34. Cather, *O Pioneers!* (1913; reprint, Boston: Houghton, 1941), 309.

35. Carol Gilligan, *In a Different Voice* (Cambridge: Harvard University Press, 1982), 163, 164.

Works Cited

Several works cited in this bibliography are available only in French, and these include *Les annales de l'Hôtel-Dieu de Québec*, recorded by Mère Juschereau; *La vie de la Mère Catherine de Saint Augustin*, by Paul Ragueneau; and *Un Outre-mer au XVIIème siècle*, by La Hontan. Both *Les annales* and *La vie de la Mère Catherine* are written in archaic French and are not in wide circulation. To the best of my knowledge, *La vie de la Mère Catherine* can only be obtained commercially, in a reprint form of the original 1671 text, from the Hôtel-Dieu in Quebec City, Quebec. I wish to thank Marshall Olds, of the Department of Modern Languages at the University of Nebraska – Lincoln, for help in translating passages cited in my own study.

Fiction and Letters

Cather, Willa. *Alexander's Bridge*. 1912. Reprint. Lincoln: University of Nebraska Press, 1977.

———. *Collected Short Fiction*. Edited by Virginia Faulkner. Lincoln: University of Nebraska Press, 1970.

———. *Death Comes for the Archbishop*. 1927. Reprint. New York: Vintage Books, 1971. In the U.K., published by Virago Press, 1981.

———. *Lucy Gayheart*. 1935. Reprint. New York: Vintage Books, 1976.

———. *A Lost Lady*. 1923. Reprint. New York: Vintage Books, 1972.

———. *My Ántonia*. 1918. Reprint. Boston: Houghton Mifflin Company, 1977.

———. *My Mortal Enemy*. 1926. Reprint. New York: Vintage Books, 1954.

———. *Not Under Forty*. 1936. Reprint. Lincoln: University of Nebraska Press, 1988.

———. *Obscure Destinies*. 1932. Reprint. New York: Vintage Books, 1974.

———. *The Old Beauty and Others*. 1948. Reprint. New York: Vintage Books, 1976.

———. *One of Ours*. 1922. Reprint. New York: Vintage Books, 1971.

———. *O Pioneers!*. 1913. Reprint. Boston: Houghton Mifflin Company, 1941.

———. *The Professor's House*. 1925. Reprint: New York: Vintage Books, 1973.

———. *Sapphira and the Slave Girl*. 1940. Reprint. New York: Vintage Books, 1968.

———. *Shadows on the Rock*. 1931. Reprint. New York: Vintage Books, 1971.

———. *The Song of the Lark*. 1915. Reprint. Boston: Houghton Mifflin Company, 1983.

———. Letter to Zoe Akins. 20 April 1922. Huntington Library, San Marino, California.

————. Letter to DeWolfe Howe. 11 December 1931. Houghton Library, Harvard University.

————. Letter to Sarah Orne Jewett. 24 October 1908. Houghton Library, Harvard University.

————. Letter to Viola Roseboro. 9 November 1940. University of Virginia Library.

Hawthorne, Nathaniel. *Selected Short Stories.* Edited by Alfred Kazin. Greenwich, Conn.: Fawcett Publications, Inc., 1966.

Jewett, Sarah Orne. *The Country of the Pointed Firs and Other Stories.* 1896. Reprint. Garden City, N.Y.: Doubleday Anchor Books, 1956.

————. *The Queen's Twin and Other Stories.* Boston: Houghton Mifflin Company, 1899.

————. *The Letters of Sarah Orne Jewett.* Edited by Richard Cary. Waterville, Maine: Colby College Press, 1967.

Critical Works, Essays, and Literary Biographies

Ammons, Elizabeth. "Going in Circles: The Female Geography of Jewett's *Country of the Pointed Firs.*" *Studies in the Literary Imagination* 16 (Fall 1983): 83–92.

Bohlke, L. Brent, ed. *Willa Cather in Person.* Lincoln and London: University of Nebraska Press, 1986.

Bloom, Edward A. and Lillian D. "*Shadows on the Rock:* Notes on the Composition of a Novel." *Twentieth Century Literature* 2 (July 1956): 70–85.

Brown, E. K., and Leon Edel. *Willa Cather: A Critical Biography.* 1953. Reprint. Lincoln and London: University of Nebraska Press, 1987.

Brown, Marion Marsh, and Ruth Crone. *Only One Point of the Compass: Willa Cather in the Northeast.* Danbury, Conn.: Archer Editions press, 1980.

Busch, Beverly Gail. *The Nature and Extent of the Influence of Sarah Orne Jewett on Willa Sibert Cather.* Ph.D. diss. Drew University (Madison, N.J.), 1986. Ann Arbor: UMI, 1986. 8616862.

Cather, Willa. *Willa Cather on Writing.* 1920. Reprint. Lincoln and London: University of Nebraska Press, 1988.

Donovan, Josephine. *New England Local Color Literature: A Women's Tradition.* New York: Frederick Ungar Publishing Co., 1983.

Fiddyment Levy, Helen. *Fiction of the Home Place.* Jackson Miss. and London: University Press of Mississippi, 1992.

Gilligan, Carol. *In a Different Voice.* Cambridge: Harvard University Press, 1982.

Lee, Hermione. *Willa Cather: Double Lives.* New York: Pantheon Books, 1989.

Lewis, Edith. *Willa Cather Living: A Personal Record.* 1953. Reprint. Lincoln and London: University of Nebraska Press, 1976.

Murphy, John J. "*Shadows on the Rock:* Cather's Medieval Refuge." *Renascence* 15 (Winter 1963): 76–78.

Nelson, Robert J. *Willa Cather and France: In Search of the Lost Language.* Urbana and Chicago: University of Illinois Press, 1988.

O'Brien, Sharon. *Willa Cather: The Emerging Voice*. New York: Oxford University Press, 1987.

Roman, Margaret. *Sarah Orne Jewett: Reconstructing Gender*. Tuscaloosa and London: The University of Alabama Press, 1992.

Romines, Ann. "The Hermit's Parish: Jeanne Le Ber and Cather's Legacy from Jewett." *Cather Studies* 1 (1990): 147–58.

———. *The Home Plot: Women, Writing and Domestic Ritual*. Amherst: University of Massachusetts Press, 1992.

Rosowski, Susan J. *The Voyage Perilous: Willa Cather's Romanticism*. Lincoln and London: University of Nebraska Press, 1986.

Sergeant, Elizabeth Shepley. *Willa Cather: A Memoir*. 1953. Lincoln and London: University of Nebraska Press, 1963.

Skaggs, Merrill Maguire. *After the World Broke in Two: The Later Novels of Willa Cather*. Charlottesville and London: The University Press of Virginia, 1990.

Slote, Bernice, ed. *The Kingdom of Art: Willa Cather's First Principles and Critical Statements, 1893–1896*. Lincoln and London: University of Nebraska Press, 1966.

Stouck, David. *Willa Cather's Imagination*. Lincoln and London: University of Nebraska Press, 1975.

Woodress, James. *Willa Cather, A Literary Life*. Lincoln and London: University of Nebraska Press, 1987.

Historical Sources

De Brumath, Adrien Leblond. *Bishop Laval*, in *The Makers of Canada*. Toronto: Morang & Co., Ltd., 1910.

Faillon, Étienne. *The Christian Heroine of Canada; or, Life of Miss LeBer*. Montreal: John Lovell, 1861.

The Jesuit Relations and Allied Documents: Travels and Explorations of the Jesuit Missionaires in New France, 1610–1791. Edited by Reuben Gold Thwaites, Secretary of the State Historical Society of Wisconsin. Cleveland: The Burrows Brothers Company, 1900.

La Hontan, Louis Armand d'Arce, Baron de. *Un outre-mer au XVIIeme siècle*. Paris: Plon-Nourrit et Cie., 1900.

Marshall, Joyce, trans. and ed. *Word from New France: The Selected Letters of Marie de l'Incarnation*. Toronto: Oxford University Press, 1967.

Parkman, Francis. *Count Frontenac and New France Under Louis XIV*. 2 vols. Part 5 of *France and England in North America*. Boston: Little, Brown, and Company, 1897.

———. *The Jesuits in North America*. 2 vols. Part 2 of *France and England in North America*. Boston: Little, Brown, and Company, 1897.

———. *The Struggle for a Continent*. Edited by Pelham Edgar. Boston: Little, Brown, and Company, 1907.

Ragueneau, Paul. *La vie de la Mère Catherine de Saint Augustin.* 1671. Reprint. Québec: Hôtel-Dieu de Québec, 1923.

Saint-Ignace, Jeanne Franc de la Ferté, Mère Juschereau. *Les annales de l'Hôtel-Dieu de Québec.* Québec: Hôtel-Dieu de Québec, 1939.

Scott, Abbé Henri A. *Bishop Laval,* in *The Makers of Canada* (Anniversary Edition). Toronto: Oxford University Press, 1926.

Index